Praise for *Tech Like a PIRATE*

Tech Like a PIRATE is a must-have for any educator who wants to demand better engagement and learning from technology use.

—Alice Keeler, author, speaker, and math educator

Matt Miller has established himself as America's go-to educator for practical ed tech practices for the classroom. In *Tech Like a PIRATE*, he skips the buzzwords and goes straight into what teachers can do to level up their use of tech, and he does so in an inviting way, so no teachers will ever feel judged.

—Noah Geisel, teacher, writer,
ACTFL Language Teacher of the Year

Matt's call to embrace the "adventure awaiting us on the high seas" is an invitation to us all to make learning fun again. And, like any captain worth his salt, Matt provides his crew with practical, innovative, and just plain fun instructional strategies. His creative energy never ceases to both amaze and deliver, and we see it here again in *Tech Like a PIRATE*.

—Stephanie DeMichele, digital learning designer and coach

Matt Miller has been a pioneer in changing the way educators view technology and the impact it can have on improving student-learning outcomes. With *Tech Like a PIRATE*, Matt takes it to another level by providing teachers with techniques and strategies to utilize technology to create deeply meaningful experiences for every learner.

—Jesse Lubinsky, chief learning officer, Ready Learner One

Tech Like A PIRATE has something special to offer whether you are a new or veteran teacher, novice or tech wizard. Miller provides plenty of solutions that keep the focus where it belongs—on content.

—Catherine Day, social studies teacher

From gaming experiences to virtual explorations and video-production alternatives, Matt Miller's *Tech Like a PIRATE* offers a simple and stimulating approach to leveraging available technology in the classroom.

—**Omar López and Fely García-López,**
Apple Distinguished Educators

This will be a well-worn book with sticky notes, tabs, and many, many notes in the margins! This is THE book I know I will have near me as I plan, using true technology integration in my lessons.

—**Krista Harmsworth, fifth-grade teacher**

Matt's examples may tie directly to specific tools; however, he explains that the thoughtful creation of the experience, not the tool or the technology, is key. This mantra rings true throughout this book: don't do tech for tech's sake.

—**David Platt, teacher and technology coach**

As a veteran classroom teacher, the things that I look for most in a professional text are fresh ideas and practical ways to incorporate them. Matt Miller offers both in abundance in *Tech Like a PIRATE*.

—**Gina Ruffcorn, fifth-grade teacher,**
technology integrationist

Tech Like a PIRATE is a great book for teachers at all levels, from the tech weary to the technology gurus! What I love about the book is that it strikes a perfect balance between inspiring teachers to be true mavericks and giving them practical ways to leverage technology NOW.

—**Scott Titmas, technology integration specialist**

Bringing a human-centered approach to teaching in a digital world, Matt Miller's *Tech Like a PIRATE* reminds us of the power of communication, collaboration, and empathy for others. If you are ready for a change, even if it means failing a few times, *Tech Like a PIRATE* is a great guidebook for starting your journey!

—**Rayna Freedman, fifth-grade teacher, MassCUE president**

Matt Miller's conversational writing style, engaging storytelling, and seemingly bottomless well of knowledge about how to winningly integrate tech into your teaching practice can take you to new and successful places as an educator. And as a bonus, reading Miller's book is almost as fun as using his tips!

—Dan Tricarico, author of *The Zen Teacher: Creating, Focus, Simplicity, and Tranquility in the Classroom*

Student engagement is EVERYTHING! Matt Miller does a phenomenal job of explaining the importance of capturing the attention of your students, promoting an authentic learning experience, and handling all of the hiccups along the way.

—Joe and Kristin Merrill, teachers and authors of *The InterACTIVE Class*

For the tech expert or noob, this book is full of ideas about how to maximize the impact on learning that technology can have in the classroom. You will learn creative ways to use tech tools and apps in order to create meaningful and memorable experiences for your students.

—Craig Klement, RTI facilitator

Tech Like a PIRATE is proof that technology can be used for way more than skill and drill. Matt Miller provides step-by-step, easy to follow instructions that any teacher can use.

—Amber Harper, edtech consultant and creator, Burned-In Teacher

Matt encourages you to be a VIP guest on the expedition of technology integration so that by the last page, you're able to "call the ball" on the lessons in your classroom and become an admirable maverick teacher!

—Evan Mosier, technology innovator

Tech Like a PIRATE isn't just a book full of theory and anecdotes. It contains tons of ideas you can use right away. Matt includes the resources you need (and want!) to be able to start implementing these activities in your class right away.

—Karly Moura, tech TOSA and computer-science teacher

This book is full of inspiration, ideas, and stories from real educators making learning powerful with technology. Matt shares his heart and passion to help make each of us better.

—Mandi Tolen, math teacher, Google Certified Innovator

The goal of every educator is to enrich their students' lives by imparting knowledge and sparking a passion for learning. Matt helps push us to slay our doubt and overcome roadblocks that may keep us from creating experiences that amplify learning.

—Lance McClard, elementary-school principal

Tech Like a PIRATE

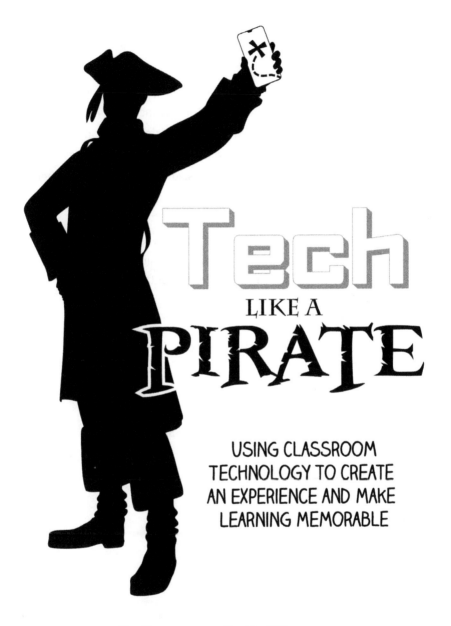

Tech
LIKE A
PIRATE

USING CLASSROOM
TECHNOLOGY TO CREATE
AN EXPERIENCE AND MAKE
LEARNING MEMORABLE

Matt Miller

Tech Like a PIRATE: Using Classroom Technology to Create an Experience and Make Learning Memorable
© 2020 Matt Miller

This book is available at special discount when purchased in quantity for educational purposes or as premiums, promotions, or fundraisers. For inquiries and details, contact the publisher at books@daveburgessconsulting.com.

Published by Dave Burgess Consulting, Inc.
San Diego, CA
DaveBurgessConsulting.com

Library of Congress Control Number: 2020935815
Paperback ISBN: 978-1-951600-20-4
E-book ISBN: 978-1-951600-21-1

Cover and interior design by Liz Schreiter

To all the real maverick
teachers, the ones who faced
pressure but still did what
they knew was best for kids.
You're the real risk-takers. Your
students thank you. I thank you.
And the world thanks you.

CONTENTS

1   INTRODUCTION: RESHAPING THE INFORMATION ECONOMY

4   CHAPTER 1: TECH LIKE A PIRATE, TEACH LIKE A MAVERICK

18 CHAPTER 2: EXPERIENCES, NOT APPS

34 CHAPTER 3: VIDEO (AND AUDIO) KILLED THE CHALKBOARD STAR

46 CHAPTER 4: ALL THE WORLD'S A GAME, AND WE ARE ALL PLAYERS

60 CHAPTER 5: FROM FOUR THOUSAND MILES TO FOUR INCHES

74 CHAPTER 6: BRAIN-FRIENDLY, INSTAGRAM-WORTHY LEARNING

88 CHAPTER 7: CHARTING THE COURSE TO A LEARNING EXPEDITION

98 CHAPTER 8: LEARNING WITH NEW FRIENDS AROUND THE WORLD

112 CHAPTER 9: SLAYING DOUBT AND ROADBLOCKS

126 AFTERWORD: TAKE THE MAVERICK TEACHER CREED

133 REFERENCES

137 ACKNOWLEDGMENTS

139 ABOUT THE AUTHOR

INTRODUCTION:

RESHAPING THE

INFORMATION ECONOMY

Urinals and toilet stalls: they have something to teach us about teaching.

In recent years, we've seen something new in public restrooms: advertisements. They're on the wall above a urinal or on the doors of toilet stalls. Why? You're a captive audience. Someone realized that your eyes were going to be fixed on that spot for a short period of time. (Unless you're checking social media while you're doing your business. But you wouldn't do that . . . or would you?) So they sold a mini billboard to place there.

Restroom advertising counts on your attention. And attention is hard to get these days. Notifications keep our cell phones buzzing and dinging, begging us to look at them. Social media is designed to keep our eyes on it—and our fingers scrolling. Online videos and TV use short scenes and segments so we won't click away.

It's hard for advertisers and social media to keep our attention. It's infinitely harder for us to retain attention in the classroom! I'll bet you've seen the results: glazed-over eyes, easily distracted students. Plus, when teaching's perceived as a drag by our students, it weighs on teachers. This sense of drudgery has contributed to a massive teacher shortage in the United States. "There is no sign that the large shortage of credentialed teachers—overall, and especially in high-poverty schools—will go away," write researchers in an Economic Policy Institute study (Garcia and Weiss 2019).

This raises an important question: how can we expect students to remember what we want them to remember when class is so forgettable?

Let's ditch the forgettable and embrace the memorable. When class is memorable, the classroom atmosphere is electric. Students enter the flow state described by psychologist Mihaly Csikszentmihalyi (1997) where their focus causes them to lose track of time and their surroundings. Learning is fun—for students and teacher!

It's all about the lens we see learning through. If our focus is *we have to learn this* or *it's on the test,* it's drudgery. But looking at class through the lens of memorable experience can transform everything! A response to a writing prompt becomes a live news report from the scene. Being asked to demonstrate your two main takeaways feels more like recording a fun YouTube video to share with friends. The question becomes: *What lens will you look through today to make class memorable?*

When we have our students' full attention, they're learning in powerful ways they weren't before. Memorable teaching. You don't even need to put anything in a toilet stall to get it.

TECH LIKE A
PIRATE,
TEACH LIKE A
MAVERICK

Sit down. **Listen** to the teacher. Do this worksheet. Read this chapter and answer the questions at the end. Some of the traditional teaching practices we've used for decades just don't get the results they once did. When we add up everything we do in class, it feels like 2 + 2 + 2 + 2 + 2 = 5. It's a lot of work without much to show for it.

What if we could flip that script? What if it felt like 2 + 2 + 2 + 2 = 13? What if we were surprised at how effective our teaching was and couldn't put our finger on the reason?

Positivity, emotion, and play can play a powerful role in our lives—and definitely in our classrooms. This is borne out by an expanding body of research. We're 31 percent more productive when our brains are in a positive state rather than in a neutral or negative state (Achor 2011). Emotional events often attain a privileged status in memory (LaBar and Cabeza 2006), and, according to the National Institute for Play, "Long-term studies under way indicate that play-based learning with playful teachers heightens overall long term performance."

That's just scratching the surface. Positivity, emotion, and play are at the heart of engaging students in class, and they make a statement. Student engagement isn't silliness that defeats true academic work. It can be a catalyst to the learning of our dreams. Making learning fun can be dismissed as fluff, nonsense, or a barrier to true learning. When fun doesn't enhance the learning in some way, it can indeed leave us spinning our wheels. But we can look at learning through a fun *lens*! Use a compelling story or a favorite app—anything that puts the lesson of the day in a new light will grab students' attention. When we get the lens right, we can transform a drab, lifeless lesson into exciting territory. For instance, what would Marie Curie's Twitter feed have looked like as she experimented with radiation? What would text messages between Brutus and Cassius have looked like before they betrayed Caesar? Would they have shown remorse afterward?

Fun doesn't stand in the way of learning. On the contrary, it is the path to the learning of our dreams.

THE POWER OF THE PIRATE

In 2012, Dave Burgess published *Teach Like a PIRATE*, in which he described the success he'd had with PIRATE teaching. These six characteristics make up his method:

Passion: Feeling passionate about teaching, even if you're not passionate about the subject you're teaching

Immersion: Being fully present and fully at attention in the moment with your students

Rapport: Connecting with students on a personal level to build a safe, fun environment

Ask/analyze: Asking the right questions about your teaching ideas and constantly analyzing their effectiveness

Transformation: Rethinking what's possible in the classroom to break down barriers

Enthusiasm: Harnessing this most powerful tool in the classroom to create high-impact teaching

I got my copy of *Teach Like a PIRATE* in 2015 as a birthday gift. (Yes, I'm that kind of teaching geek. I ask for education books for my birthday! I still have that copy—coffee stains, worn cover, damaged corners, and all.) It changed my thinking about teaching almost immediately. My brain reeled when I asked myself Burgess's most provocative question: "If your students didn't have to be there, would you be teaching in an empty room?"

Then there's this line—it stuck with me the most then and it still speaks to me now: "Don't just teach a lesson. Create an experience!"

By itself, a lesson isn't an experience. Imagine someone says, "I want to teach you a lesson." What do you do? Do you lean in? Or do you fake an important phone call to get away as fast as you can? We're generally not excited about being taught a lesson. But we're always up for an experience. An experience is memorable. It engages the senses—sight, smell, hearing, taste, touch. It piques our interest. It lets our vivid imagination take us on an adventure. An experience charges our emotions, leaving us wanting more.

DON'T JUST TEACH A
LESSON. CREATE AN

Experience!

—Dave Burgess

Teach Like a PIRATE

I read through the stories, suggestions, and hooks for engaging teaching in *Teach Like a PIRATE*, and I kept returning to the same epiphany: so many of the book's ideas could be enhanced with technology—free digital tools and tech that many schools had readily available in classrooms.

Many teachers had all the components for a memorable, techy learning experience in front of them. They just couldn't see how to assemble them to build something bigger. Something more memorable—and more effective.

I didn't realize it at the time, but I started writing this book back in 2015, when I first read *Teach Like a PIRATE*. It fit perfectly next to *Ditch That Textbook*, my blog-turned-book, where I write about the role of classroom tech in creating meaningful learning.

PIRATES AND TECHNOLOGY? YES!

In my eleven years teaching high school Spanish, English, and journalism, I've always looked for ways that tech could add to the learning experience. Hearing from other educators about how they've approached this has only confirmed my commitment to centering technology in the classroom. It's amazing what it allows us to do:

- We can talk face-to-face with experts and other classrooms like ours all over the world with video calls.
- We can share our work widely with authentic audiences through websites and podcasts.
- We can blur the border of the digital world and the real world through augmented reality.
- We can make learning visible, showing what's in our brains, with graphic design tools.
- We can create audio and video with superb production quality.

When tech is centered, students still learn. But they also develop vital skills—technical skills, communication, creativity—that will serve them later, in the workforce.

Classroom tech can help make learning fun, too. That's the heart of this book: we can weave student engagement and tech like a tapestry to create an experience that amplifies student learning.

WHEN RISK-TAKING IS WORTH IT

Near the top of my list of guilty pleasures is *Top Gun*, a classic film of the 1980s. I rarely pass up an opportunity to watch it. It chronicles the journey of Pete Mitchell, a US Navy fighter pilot with the call sign Maverick. Maverick's superior skills earn him a seat in the navy's advanced combat fighter school, known as Top Gun.

When Maverick arrives for his Top Gun training, the school's instructors find that he's no textbook-compliant student. Maverick is a risk-taker. His combat tactics are unconventional. For example, in a training flight, he battles against Jester, one of his instructors. Jester approaches Maverick's plane from the rear, the optimal place to be in a dogfight between two planes. Maverick tries the traditional moves to shake Jester off his tail, but to no avail. Then, in the moment, Maverick imagines a move that would catch Jester completely off guard. In the middle of this high-speed pursuit, Maverick decides to pitch the nose of his plane straight up and slam on the brakes, causing Jester to pass by and put Maverick in the better tactical position.

Now Maverick has Jester right where he wants him. Jester is scrambling for his life. When his skills can't save him, Jester does what only an instructor can do in a training flight. He dives below the "hard deck," the minimum safe altitude, effectively taking the competition out of bounds and ending it before Maverick can defeat him.

Maverick, however, won't have it. He follows Jester out of bounds, flying dangerously low into the California mountains, and takes his shot. Maverick celebrates his victory over Jester.

When Maverick and his partner Goose reach the ground, the instructors aren't celebrating. They chew Maverick out for breaking protocol and putting lives in danger. Maverick leaves the office with regrets.

Among themselves, though, the instructors know they've witnessed greatness. Maverick has an improvisational, creative way of flying that they've never seen. He has a talent for looking at the risk-to-reward ratio and knowing when a risk is worth taking.

Here's how Maverick decided whether a risk was worth taking. He sized up the situation. He weighed the possible options and each option's outcomes. He decided whether the potential benefits were worth the risk. Then he acted.

It's not getting results.

There HAS to be a better way!

Oh, this idea would be cool!

It's so risky, though. What if I fail?

When we think about the risk-to-benefit ratio in the classroom, it looks more like this:

- We find something about our class that we're not satisfied with.
- We decide that we're ready for a change.
- We start to brainstorm better ways of doing things.
- When we come to a solution, we worry about failing.

We educators tend to be a skittish sort when it comes to failure. (That's interesting, because we encourage our students to try new things and risk failure every single day.) Risk scares us. It keeps us from pursuing our best ideas because, we tell ourselves, something might go wrong.

But what if those things that feel risky aren't so risky at all? What if our fears had very little substance?

It's time to reframe the term *risk*.

You know what doesn't feel risky? The status quo. Education as expected. Talking at students. Marching chapter by chapter through a textbook. Assigning mindless worksheets. *Teachers have taught this way for ages. It isn't going to rock the boat or ruffle anyone's feathers. If we teach this way, we can fly under the radar, avoid parent phone calls, receive satisfactory evaluations, and keep our jobs.* So goes our inner script, even if we're not always even aware of it.

Teaching to the status quo feels safe. But is it safe? What if it doesn't get results? And what if we continue to teach using the same old techniques even though we know they're not getting great results?

Seen in this light, the status quo is not safe, but *risky*.

The definition of *risk* is a situation involving exposure to danger. Teaching that *feels* safe, but where students are less likely to learn, is risky. It's even, in its way, dangerous. Anything we do that doesn't help students realize their potential is dangerous. Risky. A wasted opportunity.

Safe, comfortable teaching is simply risky teaching.

Let's take it back to our *Top Gun* analogy. As a fighter pilot, Maverick could have relied on the "safe" combat tactics, the ones that other fighter pilots used. But against Jester, the same old tactics would have led to Maverick's demise.

For Maverick, safe flying was risky flying. Jester was going to beat him.

For us, safe teaching is risky teaching. If playing it safe isn't getting us results, we can't keep doing what we know doesn't work—even if change makes us comfortable.

WHEN RISK-TAKING IS SAFE

If safe teaching is risky teaching, what should we do? If traditional teaching isn't getting us the results we seek, breaking tradition is the safest thing we can do. Taking some risks.

Taking risks means we must try new ideas that aren't guaranteed to succeed. Let's go back to that thought process so many of us know all too well:

1. This lesson just isn't getting results.
2. There *must* be a better way.
3. Oh, this idea would be cool!
4. But what if I try this and it fails?

IS FAILURE REALLY FAILURE?

As we've seen, we can make better decisions if we're clear on our definitions. We just used the word *fail*. We asked, *What happens if it fails?* So let's define what we mean by *failure* here. Let's say that failure is when we try something new and it doesn't achieve the results we expect. It fails to meet our goals. Failure doesn't sound so scary when we define it, does it?

What if we do fail when we take risks? What if we try and just don't get the results we want?

A few things happen:

1. We probably aren't any worse off than when we were sticking with "safe teaching." What you were doing before wasn't getting results, either. That's the whole reason you went through that four-step thought process above in the first place!
2. When we see failure as a dead end, it's crippling. We can't see it that way, though. We must see failure as a way forward. That makes it empowering. Use the word FAIL as an acronym: first attempt in learning.

3. Failure lets us make progress the way a scientist does. When scientists study something, they hypothesize their idea and test it out. If it's a success, they use those results to move forward and strategize. If it's a failure, they analyze the results to improve for the next time. We can view ourselves as teacher-scientists: either we'll succeed or we'll learn how we can improve.

Your failures aren't really failures. *They're data. Your failures are data.* And you can use that data to do better in the future. A good scientist wouldn't scrap valuable data by giving up! Avoid saying to yourself, "I'll never do that again." Instead, let's just add a couple of words. Instead, say, "I'll never do it *that way* again." Thinking "never again" is a dead end. It stops us in our tracks. "Never *that way* again" is empowering. It provides a way forward.

I'LL NEVER DO THAT AGAIN.
(with "IT WAY" and "THAT" inserted)

We identify what's ineffective in our classroom. We try something new that has tremendous potential. Our failures aren't really failures if we learn something from them. Our successes are leaps and bounds better than the "tried and true," ordinary way of doing things. And we've created a class that students want to come to, where we have their rapt attention and they're engaged.

Does this "risky" teaching sound risky after all? Taking some risks in our teaching is actually one of the safest things we can do.

THINGS TO KNOW BEFORE READING THIS BOOK

In this book, we'll dive deep into seven principles through which tech can create an amazing, effective learning experience. Here's what you'll get:

- Plenty of examples you can use right away or modify for your own classroom
- Stories from practicing educators who are using these tactics
- The big picture, the "why?" for using them
- The inspiration you need to propel yourself forward into enthusiastic action

Plus you'll get some new hooks! In *Teach Like a PIRATE*, Dave Burgess shared student engagement hooks you can use—with questions to ask yourself—to boost the "wow" factor of class. *Tech Like a PIRATE* adds new hooks to the PIRATE collection!

Keep the following in mind as you read this book:

1 Apps change. Apps disappear. If a particular one doesn't exist by the time you read this book, never fear! Figure out what makes your targeted activity tick. Then do your best to find an alternative app. By the same token, some of my instructions on how to use apps aren't future-proof, but don't worry! You might need to improvise, but an app's core features—the experiences it makes possible—aren't likely to change all that much. Remake the activities I suggest for your purposes and your content.

My examples are heavy on Google tools—specifically Google Slides. I've made that choice because lots of schools have access to the G Suite tools or similar Microsoft Office tools. The versatility of Google Slides and PowerPoint lets us create—and share our creations far and wide. Many examples I give using a Google tool can be transferred to an equivalent Microsoft Office tool (e.g., Google Docs to Microsoft Word, Google Slides to PowerPoint).

Lots of links are included in this book. I'll do my best to make sure all the links stay live and updated. However, after a book is published, sometimes all of that becomes impossible. If a link isn't working, sometimes a simple Google search will do. You're also free to contact us via the Ditch That Textbook website (DitchThatTextbook.com).

This book is all about swashbuckling, adventurous, tech-infused teaching and learning! What it's not, though, is an invitation to the other kind of piracy: stealing. That goes for music, media, software, and any other materials. Let's focus on using information and media ethically. But do feel free to pillage all of the tools, hooks, and exercises you find in this book and make them your own!

There's adventure awaiting us on the high seas. Are you ready to tech like a PIRATE?

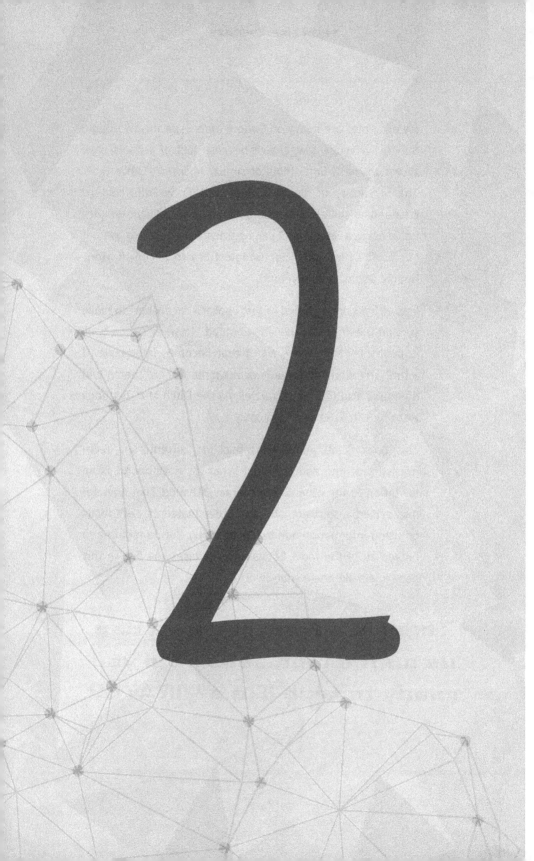

EXPERIENCES,
NOT APPS

In February 2014, the Vine craze started to creep and twist its way into my high school Spanish classroom.

It was the latest social media platform to catch fire with my students. I remember when Myspace accounts started to pop up. (I was friends with Myspace Tom! Well, so was everyone.) Then Facebook. Then Twitter. Then I heard students chatter about Vines, giggling as they watched on their smartphones between classes.

Vine was a looping-video app—now defunct—that let users record and watch six-second videos on repeat, over and over and over again. Video content was as random as the creators (called Viners). Awkward dance routines. Funny one-liners. People dressed as unicorns. Backflips. The videos were glimpses into real life, into what makes us smile and laugh and snort. My students were hooked.

When some teachers hear about their students' new favorite app, their first reaction is to try to clamp down. When there's a new app craze, I see it as an opportunity. Why are my students obsessed?

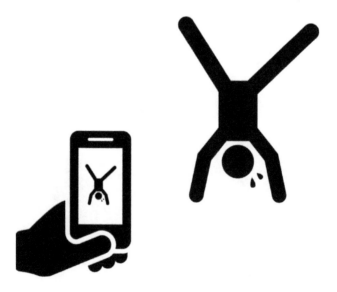

What's the hook that keeps them coming back? Most importantly, can I use the app's concept as a springboard for creating a new experience in my classroom?

It knew it was time to claim Vine's appeal for educational gain. (Of course, I know what kids say: adults ruin the great social platforms. When too many of us show up, it's time to find something else!)

One day I asked my students if they knew about Vines. Some looked offended that I'd even ask.

"So," I asked, "what if we created Vines as part of class?"

Instantly I had their rapt attention. Making Vines in class? Their minds raced for a moment. *This doesn't make sense,* they surely thought. *Teachers hate social media. They're always telling us to put our phones away. Is Mr. Miller* really *going to let us use them?*

Well, yes and no.

Yes, we were going to make six-second videos.

Yes, we would use mobile devices to shoot them.

Yes, the videos would resemble Vines. (Kind of.)

No, we weren't going to use the Vine app.

At first, I did want to use the Vine app. But I realized there were good reasons *not* to do this. The app was rated 17+ on Apple's App Store, putting it out of reach for most of my students. Some Vine videos had explicit content. Plus, the thought of all of the usernames and passwords and accounts to keep up with gave me a headache.

Then it dawned on me. It wasn't the app I was after. It was the experience. I wanted students to have the *experience* of using Vine, but without using the Vine app itself.

So we started shooting "Vines" featuring vocabulary words. Students planned how they would spend their precious six seconds. They wanted to squeeze in as much comedy, as much fun, as much *wow* as possible to impress their friends. And, of course, they had to include the chosen vocabulary word in the video.

The lesson created a lot of buzz! Students loved creating the vocab videos. It was the proof of concept that I'd hoped for. The problem was that our six classroom iPads just weren't up to the task yet. Creating, sharing, and viewing the videos was not as easy as I'd hoped. Plus, I hadn't yet found the perfect tool for creating looping videos. The idea was a bit ahead of its time.

In the end, the lesson was a bit of a bust. But a new seed was planted deep inside my teacher's soul.

YOU DON'T NEED THE APP TO CREATE THE EXPERIENCE

Think about what hooks students on their favorite apps:

- Social media apps let them share their lives with an audience of their peers and keep tabs on what everyone else is doing, saying, wearing, and eating.
- Game apps challenge students and occupy their free time. Students get bragging rights when they reach higher scores than their friends.
- News apps keep them up to speed with pop culture, sports, fashion, and so on.

Interested in recreating the experience of an app like I did with Vine? It takes just a few steps:

1. Learn about the app's features. You don't have to be an expert. You need only a basic understanding and some key details.

2. Figure out what's captivating your students. Is it the social element? A creative outlet? A competition? Something hilarious? A way to develop and showcase a talent?

3. Identify some of its signature elements. Start with the logo: the colors, the shapes, the typography. Look at its interface: the buttons, the positioning of items on the screen, the lingo. Observe how students interact with the app: by tapping, swiping, shaking?

4. Start tinkering. Maybe you start with a digital tool that's familiar to you and your students, and begin adding pieces of the app to it. Maybe you seek out a new tool or site that creates a similar experience, and start tweaking it to resemble the students' favorite app.

I followed this process to effectively recreate parts of two popular apps—Instagram and Snapchat. You can use them as examples for creating your own app-inspired learning experiences.

In the Spotlight:
INSTAGRAM STORIES WITHOUT INSTAGRAM

Instagram is a social media behemoth. Its users love shooting photos and videos, applying filters to make them look just right, and sharing them with the world. It's just one of the social media and other apps that many students are familiar with.

Instagram Stories is a popular feature, and it's a great storytelling tool. Users capture brief moments of their lives in photo or video and string the images together for others to watch one by one. That's the hook for Instagram Stories: an easy-to-use tool for sharing special moments and showing some creativity at the same time.

The potential classroom uses for a feature like Instagram Stories are countless. For example, how cool would it be to show the Instagram Story Juliet would post after Romeo's demise in *Romeo and Juliet*? How cool would it be to capture a science lab with an Instagram Story?

How can we mimic the Instagram Stories experience without the app? Can we find an option that lets us avoid problems like age restrictions, firewalls, and lack of access to mobile devices? Absolutely! Let's recreate the experience with a digital tool that many students have access to: Google Slides or PowerPoint.

Many students, young and old, are familiar with it—or are familiar with programs that have a similar user interface.

This highlights an important point when selecting technology to recreate an app's experience (or do anything in the classroom). Whenever possible, use tech that students already know. You won't have to teach them a new tool and work through the learning curve. If they already know the app, program, or platform, you can get right to the business of learning.

To simulate the experience of Instagram Stories, I first created a template on Google Slides. Students can open the template, and add images and videos. When they're done, they can use presentation mode for the slides to create the Instagram Stories experience.

Want to try it?

Download the templates for your students and view step-by-step instructions at DitchThatTextbook.com/instagramstories. By the way, PowerPoint can recreate the same experience, and it's a great option if your students have greater access to Microsoft products.

The process is pretty simple. You can replicate it in your own classroom or while working with adults in professional development. Just follow these steps:

1. Choose a digital tool that fits your planned activity well. In this case, I chose Google Slides because I wanted students to add images and video, move items around, and have multiple pages (slides).

2. Design a template, simulating the app as closely as possible. In this case, I used shapes and text from Google Slides and free icons from the Noun Project (thenounproject.com). I examined each individual part of the Instagram Stories screen on the app and looked for a way to recreate it.

3. Test the process yourself to make sure students will be able use it as planned.

4. Assign the template to students. I attached the slides to a Google Classroom assignment and chose "Make a copy for each student" on the attachment. Many learning management systems (Canvas, Schoology, and others) have similar options when working with slide presentations.

5. Let students create! Have them plan out their Instagram Stories and then start adding images and videos. When they're finished, they can turn them in, but don't let the fun end there!

6. Encourage students share their work. They can show one another their stories on their own devices, share links with classmates, or even present in front of the class using a display or projector.

What would this look like in class? How could students demonstrate their skills and proficiency with Instagram Stories? Allow your mind to roam! Here are a few ideas:

- Exploring characters from a story you've read. How would they react to the story's events in an Instagram Story?
- Exploring historical figures. How would those figures show what happened in an Instagram Story?

- Replaying a science lab. How could students show various parts of the lab?
- Demonstrating a skill. How could students teach others with photos and video?
- Charting "a day in the life." How could students share what happens in their daily lives?
- Warming up for the first day/week back to school. How could students get to know one another better?
- Practicing a foreign language. How could students get repetitions in the spoken/written language?

Many students who use Instagram regularly may already think in Instagram Stories. They see their lives through that lens. They'll do or see something worth sharing—or anticipate that what's about to happen—and they'll think, *Photo or video? Selfie or not?* If their creative capacities already work this way, let's make the connection to learning. Let them catalog, create, and share what they're learning through a platform they know and love!

Tech Treasure Trove:
OTHER WAYS TO RECREATE
THE APP EXPERIENCE

Play learning games with Snapchat Snappables. These games work with Snapchat's interactive lenses that overlay your camera. In Snappables, you're interacting with a game using your camera. Here are some of the games whose experience I knew I could recreate for class—again, with Google Slides. See a full post about using Snappables at DitchThatTextbook.com/snappables.

Why? Because commas save lives. "Let's eat Grandma!" is NOT the same thing as "Let's eat, Grandma."

- **Would You Rather:** This is the classic "choose between two options" game. In this template, you provide two options: one above and one below. Students snap a picture with their webcams pointing to their chosen options. In the text box below, students justify their responses, a sim-ple addition that engages level 3 critical thinking from Webb's Depth of Knowledge (Webb 2002). Get the template at DitchThatTextbook.com/wouldyourather.

- **My Face When:** Students snap a webcam picture showing a certain emotion—without knowing what scene or event that emotion relates to. After they place their picture on the slide, they reveal what their picture describes. Example: Students snap a picture displaying the emotion "excited." They then remove the box covering up the phrase "how the world felt when the Berlin Wall fell." Get the template at DitchThatTextbook.com/myfacewhen.

- **This or That:** This game lets students choose between two options. Students drag an outline onto their choice and justify their choice in the text box below. It's sim-ilar to "Would You Rather"—and a separate game on Snapchat—but without the selfie. Get the template at DitchThatTextbook.com/thisorthat.

Conjure up a TikTok-inspired experience with video or images. Hundreds of millions of users worldwide shoot creative videos and share them with the TikTok app. There are roadblocks to classroom use, though. Terms of service rule out younger students and inappropriate content pops up in the feed. Use a Google Slides template to simulate the feel of the TikTok app. Students can add their own images and videos to it and share with one another. Get a free TikTok-like template and ideas for using it at DitchThatTextbook.com/tiktok.

Use a student collaboration platform.

There are lots of options for creating a social media–style experience in class to boost student collaboration. Because many of these tools allow students to interact with one another as much as they would on social media, they mimic the experience of social media apps. Examples include Seesaw (seesaw.me), Class Dojo (classdojo.com), Google Classroom (classroom.google.com), and learning management systems like Canvas (instructure.com/canvas) and Schoology (schoology.com). Bloomz (bloomz.net) and Remind (remind.com) allow for students to share their work social media–style.

Start class with a tweet.

Even though adults have long predominated on Twitter, lots of students still rely on it. (At least as of the publication of this book!) The beauty of Twitter, of course, is brevity. Tweets are 280 characters or less. (They used to be even briefer: 140 characters.) Hashtags help categorize and classify tweets and can serve as comic relief: #OprahApprovesThisTweet. Your students can use a template like the one at DitchThatTextbook.com/tweettemplate to speak for someone in history, from a story, or in current events.

Galileo Galilei
@TheREAL.Galileo

Follow

Solar eclipses never get old. #SolarEclipse2017

12:15 PM · 28 Aug 2017

54,442 Retweets   158,426 Likes

28K   54K   158K

Create the experience with paper. You don't necessarily need tech to create the experience you want to mimic! If it's the experience your students are hooked on, think of what creates that experience and recreate it with (gasp!) paper. Yes, paper is still relevant. It's tactile and easily manipulated. I still carry paper notebooks everywhere for that reason. Younger students may be familiar with their parents' Facebook accounts but aren't old enough to have their own. Recreate the experience by making a "Facebook post" on a piece of paper. Borrow design elements from the app or browser experience to match the look as closely as possible. You can download and print my Google Drawings template at DitchThatTextbook.com/paperfacebook.

Finding the App Experience Hook

Many of the examples in this chapter are social media–related. Favorite mobile apps come and go, but social media appears here to stay. The apps may change (and the examples used may date this book by the time you read it), but the general idea remains the same—people *love* connecting.

Now when students are obsessed with certain apps, sites, and digital experiences, we can follow the old advice: If you can't beat 'em, join 'em! Why would we even try to "beat 'em" if the experience can help us reach our learning goals?

The App Experience Hook

- What apps are your students in love with?
- What aspects of the app have captivated your students?
- How can you recreate the app—or use some of those elements in class—to create an experience?

VIDEO (AND AUDIO) KILLED THE CHALKBOARD STAR

The VCR cart was a classroom icon when I was a student. When I walked into a class and saw one plugged in at the front of the room, I knew we were in for something good! Though I was subjected to some dreadful educational videos in my time, some classics I'll never forget, from *Schoolhouse Rock!* to *This Is America, Charlie Brown.* In my high school Spanish classes, *Destinos*, a melodramatic television series, was a staple. I loved the episodes so much that, despite the show's cheesy 1980s hair and clothing, I showed it to my own students decades later.

Video has a mystical power on our minds. With it we can enter a sort of flow state, where we lose track of time and where we are. It's like we're actually *there,* in the video. In fact, videos have real effects on our bodies. Research shows that when we watch a video, our brains work in lockstep with the characters' experiences (Hasson et al. 2004). Watching videos/films can decrease our levels of stress hormones and lower blood pressure (Miller et al. 2006)—or, conversely, increase our heart rate and spike adrenaline (Braff 2011).

Video's stronghold on our lives is only growing. A 2017 study commissioned by Cisco (2019) predicts that video traffic will account for 82 percent of all consumer internet traffic by 2021. And live video is predicted to grow fifteen-fold from 2016 to 2021.

Audio is having a resurgence, thanks in large part to smart speakers like Google Home and Amazon Echo. Tens of millions of US smart-speaker users use their voices to ask Alexa, Siri, and Google to play music, calculate math problems, provide weather forecasts, and play audio content (Enberg 2018). Audio podcasts are popular, too. One in four Americans listens to podcasts (Edison Research 2020)—convenient because you can download shows on your phone and listen at any time. Listeners can turn a commute, workout, or dog-walking time into an entertainment or educational experience.

Video and audio are also an essential part of students' digital lives, whether through YouTube, other social media, or content they record and produce themselves. Today, audiovisual experience goes far beyond the days of the school VCR cart. Today's video and audio tools empower students to create and learn. They enable students to tap into their own creativity, show what they've learned, and give their audience a glimpse into their own unique selves in the process.

Tech Treasure Trove:
VIDEO WITHIN REACH

Gone are the days when creating great video required expensive, specialized equipment. Now the image-capturing tech built in to our everyday devices can produce fantastic results, and without much fuss at all. Let's look at some accessible options for incorporating video into classroom experiences.

Shoot video on a mobile device. Cell-phone cameras can shoot high-quality video, and with 45 percent of children in the United States getting their first mobile phone between the ages of ten and twelve, you should find an ample supply in your class-room (Nielsen Company 2017). Alternatively, the web-cam and microphone on laptops and Chromebooks will record video quickly and easily. Use a tool like the ClipChamp webcam recorder (clipchamp.com/en/webcam-recorder) that activates the webcam and lets you record and download, or upload to YouTube, Google Drive, or elsewhere. These tools—and others that are simi-lar—are free or "freemium" (free with paid upgrades) but work well without the paid plan.

Record video on your device's screen. Screencast videos are easy and effective. They let you record video on your computer or Chromebook, then save, download, and share. This option works well for recording slides, creating tutori-als, and making videos by mashing up images from various apps. Screencastify (screencastify.com) works brilliantly with Google Chrome. (Screencastify also offers a free one-hour online course on creating great screencasts.

Access it at screencastify.com/course/master-the-screencast.) Screencast-O-Matic (screencast-o-matic.com) is a good option if you aren't using Google Chrome or want to try something else. Both have solid free plans without paid upgrades.

Create a whiteboard video. Using an iPad? It's easy to make a video that captures you drawing on a whiteboard and speaking through the microphone. Educreations (educreations.com) and Explain Everything (explaineverything.com) are two iOS apps that let you go beyond drawing on a digital whiteboard to add text, images, documents, web pages, PowerPoint slides, and more. Not using an iPad? Use Flipgrid (flipgrid.com) to record and change it to whiteboard mode, with the webcam off and a white screen on.

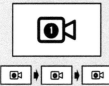

Make video with existing media. You don't even need to use a video camera to create video! Lots of great, free online tools and apps let you create flashy video by incorporating text, images, and existing video. Adobe Spark Video (spark.adobe.com) and VoiceThread (voicethread.com), to name two, let you combine photos, video clips, icons, documents, and text to make beautiful video for free.

Travel the world and beyond with green screen. Your students don't have to be limited by physical location! Green screen allows the user to drop in any background behind students in a video, transporting students virtually to another location. For the iPad, the Green Screen app by Do Ink (doink.com) lets student creativity run wild for only a few dollars in the App Store. Alternatively, video editors such as iMovie or Camtasia support green-screen effects. A quick online search for a video tutorial should get you on track.

LIGHTS, CAMERA, EXPERIENCE!

When you've selected the best option for creating video in your classroom, use it to create a memorable experience, one in which the students—and their creative capacities—are the stars of the project! Though you should give them some direction on the videos they make—to help the project seem less overwhelming—encourage students to look for inspiration in the videos they love. Let students have as much say as possible in the look of the finished product. We want students to *own* this activity, put their unique stamp on it, be proud! Encourage them to remix or recreate videos they love to showcase what they've learned in class. They can even experiment with different video formats (e.g., interviews, drama, tutorial, educational comedy, music). Remember: the last thing you want to do is give step-by-step directions. Great art isn't paint by numbers!

Here are several creative video projects with which students can wow their classmates.

- **Take virtual walking tours.** Use Google Maps Street View and a screencasting tool to take classmates on a virtual tour of places all over the world! Street View shows what life looks like at street level in full, 360-degree glory. Students can record these panoramic images using a screencast tool like Screencastify. They can walk the streets virtually, describing what they see and adding details to demonstrate their learning. If you're using Screencastify, videos will upload automatically to Google Drive, which makes submitting it to Google Classroom or a learning management system easy. See how to do this step-by-step at DitchThatTextbook.com/walkingtour.
- **Be the news anchor.** Create a basic TV news set with desk, chairs, and a backdrop. (A whiteboard will do, too.) Or create an elaborate set with decorations, wardrobe, and more!

TOP NEWS

Record with the camera on a cell phone or other mobile device, or using a webcam on a laptop or Chromebook. Students show what they've learned through the news camera lens, delivering content to viewers as if it's the evening news.

- **Host a game show.** Recreate a game show or other TV game like *Cash Cab* or "Carpool Karaoke" that brings in content from class. You can script it all out or record it off the cuff!

- **Create a how-to video segment.** Lots of YouTubers have achieved fame with great how-to videos. Tons of creative, fun examples are available for inspiration. Let students remix and borrow ideas from their favorites to create their own captivating how-to videos.

- **Get dramatic.** *The Blair Witch Project* was a movie made on a sixty-thousand-dollar budget that brought in 250 million dollars at the box office. It wasn't the best movie ever, but it

did capture the cinema world's attention. How did the creators do it? They told the story using what appeared to be raw, uncut video. Create your own horror story *Blair Witch*–style, or pretend to shoot an event in live-video style à la Facebook Live, YouTube Live, or Periscope.

- **Don't limit the fun to students! Teachers can get in on the act by creating their own videos that show their personality, entertain students, and encourage learning.** Shoot your own educational videos and make them available to students. Be sure to let yourself shine through! You are your own unique self, and believe it or not, your students are eager to see it! Get creative to catch students off guard and leave them talking. One college professor created a video that he displayed on his projector, then proceeded to talk to the recorded version of himself on-screen, to his students' bewilderment! Check it out at DitchThatTextbook.com/profvideo. I've also seen cases where a teacher starts a video and walks out of the room as a video version of the teacher appears on-screen and lets students in on a few quick secrets before the "live" teacher returns to class. Use your imagination and let your students be surprised.

A challenge can create an experience, too! Students all over North America participated in the first Slay the Mic Jr. video program in 2019. The program gave students speaking prompts on a variety of topics, like self-introduction, feelings, who they saw themselves becoming. In recording the videos, students steadily built their confidence, and over the course of a month, students could literally see a transformation in their speaking. Jam Gamble, the educator-turned-public-speaker who organized the event, says it's all about celebrating students' voices and their growing skills. "Growing up, I was often that kid who got into a lot of trouble for talking and I don't think my voice was really celebrated," she says. "This is all about celebrating." Want to get involved? Check out the #STMJRChallenge hashtag and Jam's Twitter feed (@Iamjamgamble). Or conduct your own Slay the Mic Jr. challenge! Create prompts, provide feedback, celebrate student voices, and watch your students transform.

Find more than twenty video project ideas that you can use immediately—including ten content area–specific ideas—at DitchThatTextbook.com/videoprojects.

HELPING STUDENTS FIND THEIR VOICES

Audio is popular. Podcasts were born and soon started to gain popularity after the iPod was first released in 2001. In the years since, podcasts have only continued to grow in listenership. Fifty-five percent of the US population aged twelve and over has listened to the hundreds of thousands of podcasts available (Edison Research 2020). Fans are listening on their smart speakers, with podcast apps on their phones, and through laptop speakers on internet browsers.

The traditional route to posting a podcast is to create audio, upload it to a host, and get it distributed through iTunes and other platforms. This can be complicated and expensive.

Thankfully, though, the process is getting easier all the time, and now there are simple apps to help you get your audio recorded and heard. Tools like Anchor (anchor.fm) and Podbean (podbean.com) can help your students create a class podcast (through your account and  supervised by you if they're not old enough for terms of service). I've created my own podcast with Anchor and found it to be quite easy and painless. Learn more about how to make it happen and how your students can collaborate to create a podcast by going to DitchThatTextbook.com/studentpodcast.

Once again, though, you don't need the app to create the experience! Students can create amazing audio that engages and shows their learning *without* being listed on iTunes and other podcast platforms. Synth (gosynth.com), for example, enables students to create audio and interact with one another, allowing conversations to unfold naturally, at any time or place. Synth preserves conversations for future listening, lets others participate anywhere in the world, and makes conversations searchable. Class discussions can continue and be revisited via these digital discussions, and group project conversations can happen anywhere, at any time. Students can forgo in-person meetings without forgoing the detailed discussions they need.

Finding the Audio/Video Hook

One of humans' greatest desires is to know others and be known by others in turn. Students share a piece of who they are, their personal, unique selves, when they make audio and video. When they create something truly special, its potential reach is now virtually unlimited. Student passion can ignite a spark that spreads around a community, a country, or even the world. At eleven years old, Malala Yousafzai blogged in 2009 about the oppression of the Taliban in her region of Pakistan and brought global attention to the issue, highlighting the importance of girls' education. Students of Marjory Stoneman Douglas High School in Parkland, Florida, could have stayed quiet after a shooting ravaged their school in 2018—instead they organized and raised their voices for gun control. You have to admire their courage, and their ability to affect the public conversation.

Our students all have their own powerful, unique voices. One of the greatest gifts we can give is to help them hone their voices and share their world-changing ideas. Video and audio give them an enormous, global platform for promoting meaningful change.

The Audio/Video Hook

- How can students use video tools to display their creativity?
- How can students showcase their unique personalities and talents using video to teach others?
- What can students create with video and audio that helps them make sense of new ideas in the process?
- How can students use the captivating power of audio to spread their voice and educate others?
- What can students record that will help their classmates see the world differently?
- What can you, the educator, make that will engage your students and help them see your content—and the world—differently?

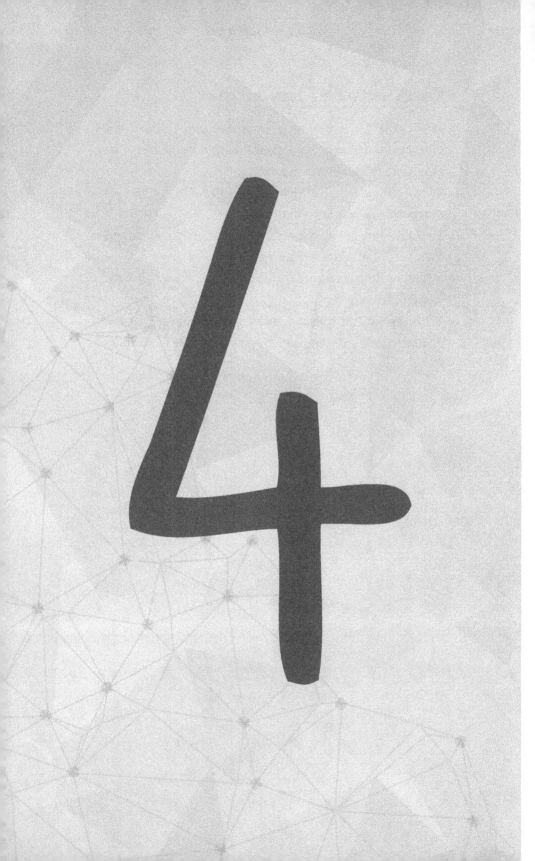

ALL THE WORLD'S A GAME, AND WE ARE ALL PLAYERS

When the Clash of Clans craze hit my school, students were pitted against students in rival armies. In this cooperative game, you build a clan of warriors and build up a stronghold to fight others off and defend your turf. On their own time, my high school students chose sides and went to battle. They gathered elixir and gold, built fortresses and walls, and beefed up their armies.

The clash didn't end at the classroom door, though. Trash talk spilled into class, with students boasting of glorious victories and epic battles, daring rival classmates to lick their wounds and come back for more.

For the most part I managed to settle them down when the bell rang. But the seed was planted in my mind. *If the students are so excited about it, how can we imitate this app to create an experience?*

In this book, technology usually creates the experience. In this case, though, the technology inspired a "real life" experience instead—a review game based on a mobile game app.

I created a Clash of Clans-inspired review game. You wouldn't guess it from the name—Ultimate Bedroom Makeover—but the Clash fingerprints were all over it. Students answered questions to earn points. They saved their points and cashed them in for items, collecting spoils they way they gathered gold and elixir in Clash of Clans. I drew a huge bank of items on one part of our whiteboard, including typical bedroom items like beds, lamps, and desks. But it also included outrageous things, like slides, swimming pools, and a Ferrari. When students bought these items with their points, they drew them into their bedroom on the whiteboard at the front of class. How the students positioned the items in their bedroom drawings was up to them, and how creatively they used their swag helped determine the winning team. At the end of class, each student voted on their favorite bedroom (without voting for themselves). Sometimes, the team that hadn't earned as many points won the game—because they'd arranged their bedrooms with serious creativity and flair.

I learned early in my teaching career that games—even individual elements of games—can motivate and inspire students to new levels. Games create motivation seemingly out of thin air, encouraging students to engage—even strive to the highest levels—when they might not otherwise. True, sometimes they're participating and striving just for the sake of a game. But they're still participating and striving—and learning.

AREN'T GAMES A WASTE OF TIME?

Jane McGonigal is the director of game research and development at the Institute for the Future, and an avid gamer. Her mantra is "play with purpose," but her experience goes much deeper than that. A game saved her life.

McGonigal suffered a severe concussion in 2009 when she hit her head in an office accident. Her symptoms lasted for weeks and led to suicidal thoughts. To battle those thoughts and keep herself focused on healing, she created a game to encourage positive actions. She called it Jane the Concussion-Slayer, but later renamed it as SuperBetter. It helped her find her way to recovery, and since then it has helped nearly half a million people achieve personal growth and tackle real-life challenges (McGonigal 2020). It's available online at superbetter.com and as an app for iOS and Android mobile devices.

Games have benefits for everyone that go beyond killing time. First, games can fight depression (Zomorodi 2016). "The opposite of play isn't work; the opposite of play is depression," she said during an interview on the Note to Self podcast. Second, a short burst of a tricky puzzle game like sudoku or Cut the Rope can provide a boost of energy and motivation. Third, games that induce a flow state can reduce anxiety or stress when played for about twenty minutes. Finally, she noted, video games can instill grit, persistence, creativity, and a sense of community. Always ask this about video games, said McGonigal: *What have you gotten better at since playing this game?*

LEARNING THROUGH GAMES

Classroom technology is a fantastic medium for playing games, creating games, and augmenting games in real life. Games can supercharge student engagement and help them learn more. We can find ideas in so many places: console video games like Nintendo Switch or PlayStation, mobile game apps like Angry Birds or Clash of Clans, or traditional board games like Monopoly and Risk. You can even find inspiration in retail rewards programs (Starbucks stars), playground games (rock paper scissors), and role-playing games (Settlers of Catan).

Use one of three approaches to choose the basic concept of a classroom game:

- **Build your own game.** Find an interesting element in an existing challenge or game (such as earning points to buy items, like in my Clash of Clans–inspired game) and tweak it to invent something new. Don't worry if it's not perfect when you start—your students can help you improve it as you play!
- **Let your students create something.** The more we turn education over to students, the more they'll own it and become lifelong learners. Let them brainstorm and come up with the best themes, rules, twists, characters, and more when adding game elements to class.
- **Steal ideas.** If the first two options don't work, stealing ideas might. Author Austin Kleon encourages you to steal like an artist. (It's not as nefarious as it sounds.) Find ideas anywhere and everywhere. Gather them. Then use them as inspiration. Mash them up into your own creation. In his book *Steal Like an Artist* (2012), Kleon writes, "Everything is up for grabs. If you don't find something worth stealing

today, you might find it worth stealing tomorrow or a month or a year from now."

Once you've gotten some ideas about game elements you'd like to steal or modify, how can you use technology to create a great gaming experience that boosts student learning, engagement, and motivation? Here are some examples:

PLAY GAMES FOR REPETITIONS

Some material we cover doesn't involve deep critical thinking. These basic things—vocabulary, state capitals, spelling words—are important but require only some repetition to assign to long-term memory. Lots of digital tools offer repetition and formative assessment in the style of a game style, such as:

- **Kahoot! (kahoot.com):** Multiple choices are displayed to students at the same time.
- **Quizizz (quizizz.com):** Multiple choices are displayed on student devices at their own pace.
- **Quizlet Live (quizlet.com/features/live):** Teams work to find the right answer using multiple devices in this collaborative flash-card game.
- **Gimkit (gimkit.com):** Students answer questions to earn points and purchase "powerups" to boost their score.
- **Flippity (flippity.net):** This platform lets you create practice games using Google Sheets.

Be sure to use these games in moderation, though. Students can go from total engagement to total boredom because of overuse. (Have you heard of Kahoot! burnout?) On the other hand, putting a new spin on a class favorite can have great benefits. A blind Kahoot! game lets teachers teach with Kahoot! instead of just reviewing with it. Similarly, there are *lots* of twists a class can put on Quizlet Live review games.

More details are available at DitchThatTextbook.com/blindkahoot.

Instead of playing all the way to 12, teams stop at 11. This way, all teams get **ELEVEN** to a full round of practice and aren't forced to stop when the winning team wins.

Players remain in their seats. They don't move to their groups. They communicate **CACOPHONY** verbally across the class. (The quieter version of this: they communicate silently across the class.)

New ways to play

QuizletLive

Ideas from Patrck McMillan (@EdTechMcMillan)
More: DitchThatTextbook.com/quizletlive

Students set up computers side by side. They line up behind their computers. **RELAY** When the game starts, they take turns looking at all the computers. They find the right answer and tag the next player to play.

Half the team stands and half sits. Standers tap a sitter's shoulder (left **TAG TEAM** or right) for the computer with the right answer. Sitter looks up and chooses the correct answer.

PLAY GAMES TO INTERACT WITH DATA

I've always loved the premise of *Family Feud*. The show asks a set of questions to one hundred people, and for each question, contestants must guess what the most popular answers are. It's great practice for students in understanding how others think, using hypothesizing and reasoning skills. You can gather your own data from students (or teachers, or others) with a Google Form to recreate this game. You can even use existing data sets (such as census data) to create the game. Add the data to my Google Slides template at DitchThatTextbook.com/familyfeud to create your own *Family Feud* game. It will help your students go beyond the data and create deeper thinking prompts for analyzing why the data are what they are.

PLAY GAMES TO IMPROVE PROBLEM SOLVING

Breakout EDU is a twist on the "escape rooms" craze. The basic premise: you're locked in a room and must solve a riddle with other captives to escape from the room. In Breakout EDU, students work to unlock the "Breakout box," which is secured with several locks. Clues and objects hidden around the room help students unlock the locks. Many teachers use Google tools like Sites and Forms to create a digital Breakout EDU–style game. Browse and play some examples at breakoutedu.com/digital. Learn how to create your own digital escape room, with a free planning guide and step-by-step instructions, at DitchThatTextbook.com/escaperooms.

USE GAMES TO MAKE REVIEWING AN EXPERIENCE

I'm a huge fan of review games. I have invented and borrowed my fair share during my teaching career. By using the technology available to you, you can enhance your review games and turn them into a memorable experience! One year, in the months before the summer Olympics, my classes played a multiday, cumulative review game called Spanish Class Olympics. I packaged several of my standard review games together in a massive review event, but I used technology to add a few special touches to make it extra memorable:

- **Music.** Right after the bell rang each day to start class, I played the traditional music the NBC television network plays during the Olympic Games: *Bugler's Dream* by Leo Arnaud. The song triggers memories and gets me in a competitive mood every time I hear it!
- **Leaderboard.** I created a template in Google to show which student group was leading the pack and updated it every day. We used three teams because the math seemed to work well for the class sizes and the arrangement of the games. The winning team for each game earned five points, second place got three points, and third place got one point.

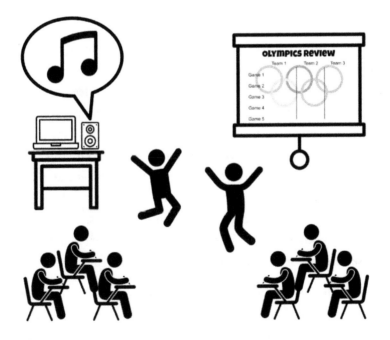

- **Games.** I picked some of our favorite digital review games (see above) and mixed them with some traditional, "real life" review games like Flyswatters, Trashketball, Row Wars, and others.

> Get details on all of these games plus a leaderboard template you can copy and use at DitchThatTextbook.com/olympicreview.

CREATING A YEARLONG GAME

Individual games can create instant student engagement. But the benefits of these games may not be long-lasting. For motivation that continues for days, weeks, or months, the game has to last longer than a day. Students need an incentive to keep playing . . . something to strive for! A cumulative game that lasts throughout the school year provides a framework for playing—and achieving!—that will keep students coming back for more.

Think of a rewards program for a store, restaurant, or other retailer you visit. For me, it's stars in Starbucks Rewards. I like Starbucks coffee, but not enough to shun all other coffee shops. What keeps me coming back is the stars. Every time I purchase something from Starbucks using my app, I earn stars. Sometimes you can earn extra stars if you purchase certain items within a certain time frame. My goal? To earn free coffee. Starbucks's goal? To get me to spend more at their stores. In yearlong cumulative games, classes need goals, and the game should build toward those goals.

In his book *Explore Like a Pirate* (2015), Michael Matera identifies several important features of a yearlong class game:

- **Theme.** Serving as the foundation to activities, items, badges, challenges, and the like, theme can be derived from a movie, an era in history, a genre of story, or other sources. What theme will most interest your students?

- **Setting.** Details of the location and time period can spark the imagination.
- **Characters.** Will your students be the characters? What kinds of characters are part of the game? Are there other characters students can interact with? Compelling characters to inhabit, cheer for, or root against can amp up student enthusiasm and really get students invested in the game.
- **Action/conflict.** What's the plotline? What are the characters striving to achieve? What will their journey look like? How does the conflict get resolved?

Carrie Baughcum, who teaches special education at an Illinois middle school, crafted her game theme carefully, creating a year-long game she calls "StarWarsopoly"—a mashup of elements from the Star Wars movies and the classic Monopoly board game. Each student starts out as a Padawan Jedi in hopes of becoming a Master Jedi. Students earn points for demonstrating positive student skills, like preparedness and time management, and twenty-first century

From the classroom of
Carrie Baughcum
Twitter:
@HeckAwesome

**REBEL
CHALLENGES**

**IMPERIAL
CHALLENGES**

More:
http://carriebaughcum.
com/bright-ideas-6-star
warsopoly-gamification

skills, like collaboration and creativity. Points can then be used to earn powers, such as that bestowed by the much-coveted lightsaber, and to buy properties that earn them rent. Different colors of lightsabers stand for different strengths students have displayed throughout the year. Baughcum explains that she layers game elements over what she's already covering, meaning that the game doesn't eat up precious instructional time.

Missouri English teacher Laura Steinbrink chose a *Marvel's Agents of S.H.I.E.L.D.* theme for all the cool secret missions and "spy stuff." Her students cocreated the theme with her. "You can add in aspects of any game, movie, or pop culture fad," she says. She builds teamwork into her game with long-lasting teams *and* special missions where team members are mixed up. When you're planning your game, she cautions, "Don't get bogged down in so many details that you never actually gamify your class." Read more about Laura's class game at DitchThatTextbook.com/gametheme.

The technology available in the classroom can deepen the experience of a long-running class game and make it especially memorable. You can integrate the design elements of the game into everything you do. Copy the colors, typography, images, and quotes. If you're using Google Classroom, create a custom header with elements from your game. Use Classcraft (classcraft.com) as a home base for managing your gamified classroom. The free version includes options like customized characters. An alternative is to use the gamification template in Google Sheets created by educator, writer, and speaker Alice Keeler. Find it at DitchThatTextbook.com/alicegamification.

Finding the Gaming Hook

Board games, mobile game apps, video games, and sports—they draw us in because we love to play. When learning turns to play, boredom transforms into bouncing, chores into chortling, drudgery into dancing. When students have feelings of elation about school and can't wait to get to class again, their minds will be open, and their hearts will be ready.

The Gaming Hook

- How can you incorporate elements of your students' beloved video games, shows, movies, and other pop culture favorites into your class?
- How can you extend the gaming challenge throughout an entire unit, semester, or year?
- How can you use a game format to make repetitions more fun?
- What challenges can you devise for your students to motivate them throughout the learning process?

FROM
FOUR THOUSAND MILES
TO
FOUR INCHES

It was just a Google Doc. I had never before seen students so fixated on a single Google Doc. But it wasn't the document itself that turned class into such a memorable experience that day. No—it was something much bigger, even profound, that drew students in.

Weeks earlier, I had introduced the students in my Spanish 3 class to some new friends. They were learning a language, too.

The difference? These friends, all seventeen or eighteen years old, like my students, lived thousands of miles away, in cosmopolitan Valencia, Spain. We lived in very rural west-central Indiana.

At first, the two classes met through a simple Skype call. We played a "Mystery Skype" game as an icebreaker. (More on that in Chapter 8.) Then we asked one another questions about daily life, like What do you eat for dinner? What kind of shoes do you wear?

During our second video call, we got down to business. It was in the most routine place—a Google Doc—where the magic started to happen. Students were put into small groups—each composed of two kids from Indiana and two kids from Valencia. We teachers provided some discussion questions and connected the group members via shared documents. The experience resembled getting to know a far-off pen pal, but digital and in real time.

As some of my students answered discussion prompts, one group started buzzing with excitement. Why? A single, turquoise-colored cursor had appeared on their screen. The cursor moved down the document, below one of the questions. Then words started to appear.

The students from Spain were in the document at the same time we were. They were typing their answers, and we saw them instantly. Real-time collaboration.

It was such a small thing. Online collaboration in documents was not groundbreaking at that time, and it isn't today.

But somehow, to us, it truly was big. Valencia, Spain, was 4,409 miles from our school. But in the digital world, we worked side by side with our Spanish friends as if we were four inches apart. It felt like a turning point. Distance wasn't an obstacle. We were free to work with, learn from, and collaborate with practically anyone at any time.

Collaboration isn't just about deciding to do group projects—it's a belief that we're better together. As technology writer David Weinberger (2011) has argued, "The smartest person in the room is the room."

Collaboration also gives students practice in four of the top attributes employers value in job candidates. According to the 2020 *Job Outlook* survey published by the National Association of Colleges and Employers (2019), problem-solving skills, the ability to work in a team, written communication skills, and leadership make the top six.

In this survey employers reveal an important truth in today's working world: Who's doing the work is less important. Working together to achieve more is what counts. We have a hard time squaring our approach with that reality in schools and classrooms, though, where we remain stubbornly attached to assigning an individual letter grade to everything students do.

Collaborative work is amazing—both exciting and productive. Students crave social interaction, after all. When they learn to work together to pursue a worthwhile goal, our classrooms are part of building the leaders the future needs, and technology can only help. Digital tools provide fertile ground for successful collaboration.

Who's doing the work is less important. **Working together** to achieve more is what counts.

In the Spotlight:
COLLABORATION GALORE IN SHARED SLIDES

The biggest appeal of social media is the connections we make with others. We have the chance to see other people's reactions to what we've shared and to learn from others. Collaborative learning creates the same experience in the classroom. Online presentation tools like Google Slides and PowerPoint Online make this possible—quick and easy, too.

To start out, create a slide presentation, making enough slides for each student (including a few extras). Then share it with students, inviting them to join the file and edit it. (Google Classroom or your learning management system is good for this. Watch a step-by-step tutorial at DitchThatTextbook.com/sharedslides.) It's a fast, low-prep activity to set up, and yields some great benefits:

- A little piece of digital real estate for every student. All students get their own slide to do their own work.
- A shared learning environment where everyone is doing their work together. Students have their own spaces, but the whole class is working together to create something bigger. Consider it a form of "crowdsourcing," where everyone does a little to achieve a lot quickly.
- An easy way to talk about what they're creating and learning. The comment feature opens up the true collaborative nature of this activity. Students check out one another's slides digitally. They engage one another there, writing comments about their thoughts, questions, and opinions.

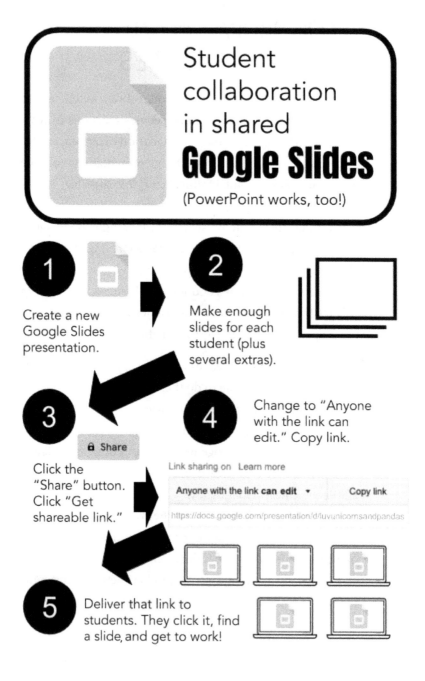

Student collaboration in shared **Google Slides**
(PowerPoint works, too!)

1 Create a new Google Slides presentation.

2 Make enough slides for each student (plus several extras).

3 Click the "Share" button. Click "Get shareable link."

🔒 Share

4 Change to "Anyone with the link can edit." Copy link.

Link sharing on Learn more
Anyone with the link **can edit** ▾   Copy link
https://docs.google.com/presentation/d/luvunicornsandpandas

5 Deliver that link to students. They click it, find a slide, and get to work!

What do they do next? The slides are literally a blank slate, so the answer is *anything!* Here are some ideas to get started with slides in class:

- **Writing prompts.** Give students a topic (or a freewrite) and ask them to write on their slides instead of in a document.
- **Brain dumps.** Let students write out everything they remember about a topic—in words, images, or both!
- **Graphic organizers.** Set up a slide with a simple graphic organizer like a Venn diagram, a fishbone diagram, or a KWL (know, want to know, learned) chart. (Examples you can copy are at DitchThatTextbook.com/graphicorganizers.) Duplicate the slide for each student and let them get started.
- **Infographics.** These visually rich creations blend text and images. (We'll talk more about them in the next chapter.) Combine icons, photos, shapes, and more with text. Learn more at DitchThatTextbook.com/infographics.
- **Comic strips.** Snap some photos with your device's webcam. Then add speech bubbles, more images, arrows . . . anything! (Again, we'll cover this further in the next chapter.) Learn more with this post I wrote with California educator Cori Orlando: DitchThatTextbook.com/comicstrips.
- **Videos.** Let students choose a video that illustrates a concept or advances a discussion in class. Students can add text to the slide to justify their choice, creating a sort of curated annotated playlist.

Once students are done working in their own slides, it's time to collaborate! They look at one another's slides and add comments. Most students are familiar with social media. Writing comments in response to something a friend has posted will be natural. In fact, you could say that many students, through frequent social media use, have spent untold hours practicing the skill of digital commentary. Let's use that to our advantage! We can borrow some of *Wikipedia's*

rules for discussion (2020) as a guide: Be polite. Assume good faith. Avoid personal attacks. Use reliable sources.

Another virtue of using shared slides? It's low-prep! Once students know what to do on their slides, your work is done and theirs begins. You've created a digital workshop for collaboration and creation with the rich materials of text, image, and multimedia. You've given students enough direction to get started but enough freedom to make the activity their own.

As they work, keep an eye on what they're doing. Give plenty of encouragement. Provide a bit of correction and redirection. But most of all, savor the one-to-one conversations and relationship building you're free to engage in. The *students* are the ones creating the experience, and you're creating a real face-to-face personal experience with them as they do it!

Tech Treasure Trove:
OTHER COLLABORATION PLATFORMS

Are slides required for collaborative work? Absolutely not! Think of the apps, websites, and digital tools that you and your class use most. Any that provide students with their own space to work and a way to comment on their peers' creations will do just as well. Slide presentations are in no way mandatory! In fact, students can do the work on individual sheets of printer paper and then swap papers to comment. Don't get tied down to the digital tool. Fall in love with the experience, and find a way to recreate that experience with a tool that suits your students best.

Here are some other formats to consider to foster digital collaboration among your students:

 **Blogging.** Blogs allow anyone to write, publish, be noticed, and interact with readers. Potential topics range from reflections to class content to freewrites to Genius Hour–style passion projects. Student blogging platforms abound, with free and paid options. Choose among Kidblog (kidblog.org), Blogger (blogger.com), Edublogs (edublogs.org), and others. Check out my own blog, where you'll find:

- Twenty ideas for solid student blogging: DitchThatTextbook.com/blogging
- Top tools, tips, and resources for getting started: DitchThatTextbook.com/bloggingbootcamp
- My blogging voyage, and how I do it (step by step): DitchThatTextbook.com/studentblogs

Maps. Create a crowdsourced map built by your students. In MyMaps (google.com/mymaps), you can drop pins onto a custom map of the world. When you click on a pin, up pops a card where you can add a title, text, clickable links, images, and videos. Essentially, each pin turns into its own multimedia presentation. Each pin can be organized into layers and given its own custom icon on the map. Working together, students can pin important locations from a country you're studying or a book you're reading. They can identify places in certain biomes, locations where important historical events took place, or epicenters of statistical data sets. Of course, discussion is an important part of the process: talking about their decisions to pin—or not to pin—and what they see in the completed map enrich the experience.

> **Twenty Ways Google's MyMaps Can Enhance Lessons in Any Class: DitchThatTextbook.com/mymaps**

YouTube. Students can certainly collaborate to create videos and upload them to YouTube. But that's not the only way to use it for collaborative learning. Students can collaborate on playlists, for example, selecting videos that represent a certain character in history, depict the location you're studying, or teach skills you want them to learn. Just share the playlist using the "Share" or "Collaborate" option. Students can add videos and even update the title and description of the playlist. Consider creating an editable online document (for example, with Google Docs or Word Online) where students can write which video they added and why it was a good addition. Then include a link to that document in the description of the playlist so students can access it easily.

Videos. Digital collaboration is much more than text. Flipgrid (flipgrid.com) is an app that lets students record short videos in response to a topic or question posed to the class. Students record videos that can be seen by their classmates. They can then leave video replies, engaging one another in further video conversation. The topics and grids (where topics live) can be shared far and wide, so that anyone around the world can participate in your discussion. Go to resources.flipgrid.com for helpful guides for teachers and students to get started.

PROMPTING OFFLINE COLLABORATION

Collaboration does not always have to be digital, of course! Preserving face-to-face communication is part of preserving our humanity. I believe we're perfectly positioned to help students maintain our humanity and our ability to relate to each other without technology. We position them very well to thrive in their work lives *and* in their personal lives—as humans!—if they can communicate both with and without technology.

Finding the Collaboration Hook

Humans are social animals. We crave learning from one another, interacting, seeing others, and being seen. Great collaboration is like a growing flower. You can't force a flower to grow. But you can ensure the best environment for it to thrive. Craft that environment. Trust that your students will make the most of it. (And if they don't, learn from the experience. Help them learn from it. Improve for next time!) What an experience you'll create when the flower of collaboration blooms into strong relationships between you and your students—or between students who didn't know each other as people before!

Here are some important tips for growing collaboration in the classroom:

- **Blend digital collaboration with face-to-face.** Communication isn't just one or the other in our real lives. Help students practice thriving in digital conversations and those in real life. Give your best suggestions—even if you don't feel like an expert on the topic!

- **Establish some ground rules.** The goal here is to create "guardrails"—like those on highways that protect you from danger. But remember that an exhaustive list of all possible "don'ts" can kill a collaborative culture in your class, send a message of mistrust, and inadvertently suggest ways students might misbehave. Instead, consider a list of "dos" that will empower students.

- **Model how to behave when things go wrong.** Expect that students will abuse the system. Instead of giving up on the activity, work with the individual student—or help the class think through the abuse. Above all, keep your cool. By keeping a level head, you're teaching students more than the curriculum; you're teaching them how to respond under pressure.

The Collaboration Hook

- How can you add a layer of interaction between students to help them see others and be seen?
- What juicy question can you ask that will get students talking?
- How can students work together to create something bigger, cooler, or more comprehensive than they could by themselves?
- Where can students use their cumulative experiences to improve learning and create an experience?

BRAIN-FRIENDLY, INSTAGRAM-WORTHY LEARNING

Billboards, magazine advertise-ments, and social media posts all have two things in common: (1) they're trying to stop us in our tracks so we'll notice something, and (2) they rely heavily on visuals.

You have an enormous billboard that can help capture your students' attention—and create an experience—in your classroom: your whiteboard or chalkboard.

Often, we'll write reminders on them. Bullet points. Important concepts from a lesson. But do we use a whiteboard to spark students' imagination? To show them what a new idea might look like? To put a smile on their faces *and* help them learn?

This was an instructional risk I took while teaching high school Spanish in my own classroom. (Whether you teach Spanish or math or second grade, there's an application here!) My students and I created stories together in Spanish to help us practice our new vocabulary and grammar. The stars of the stories were my students. We brainstormed together to settle on the next plot twist or funny setting for the story. All the while, we practiced our new material.

At first, the stories were just OK. My kids weren't running to class with enthusiasm to start the day's story. Most of them were paying attention, but some were drifting off. I wanted to take it to the next level. Then I realized that I had a huge canvas for story illustrations: the whiteboard!

When we decided on characters for the next day's story, I drew them on the board. Super-quick stick figures. As we decided on more character traits, I added some accessories, like a hat or a wig. We created the setting: a supermarket. I drew a quick building (think a house that a third grader would draw) and labeled it *supermercado*, Spanish for supermarket. Suddenly, those wandering, inattentive eyes of a few listless students were glued to the board. Part of it, I'm sure, was the introduction of something new. But part of it, I'm convinced, was that they could visualize the story.

After a full class period of story creation, laughter, and making shabby stick drawings on the board, our story was complete. Then some of the students did something I'd never expected. They asked to use their cell phones to take pictures of the drawings! Some of them even posted the drawings to their social media accounts.

My drawings were a mess. They didn't want to take pictures because I'm any kind of great artist. My poorly drawn stick figures tended to the eccentric, say one short arm and one long arm. (Sometimes, my mistakes would become embedded in the story. We had a one-armed man because my line for the arms didn't extend far enough!) Students wanted to capture the images because we had created an experience together. They captured them because they, the students, were the stars in this crazy story we had all helped to invent.

There's a reason "a picture is worth a thousand words" came to be a cliché. Visuals—including images and videos—are vivid. They connect with our brains differently than text, as Marcel Just, the director of the Center for Cognitive Brain Imaging at Carnegie Mellon University, explains (2010):

"Processing print isn't something the human brain was built for. The printed word is a human artifact. It's very convenient and it's worked very well for us for 5,000 years, but it's an invention of human beings. By contrast, Mother Nature has built into our brain our ability to see the visual world and interpret it. . . . I think it's inevitable that visual media are going to become more important in conveying ideas."

Ask yourself: How could this work in my classroom? Could I, at the very least, draw charts or graphs or diagrams to help my students understand? Could I add some fun—or something that reflects my students and their uniqueness—to what I draw on the board? Could I ask a student to illustrate for me (quickly, maybe with time limits) if I don't want to do it myself?

Tech Treasure Trove:
FINDING PICTURES WORTH A THOUSAND WORDS

If we want the brain benefits—and the wow factor! —that come from great images, we need to know where to find and create them first. Here are a few options.

Use Google Images. Searching Google Images without any filters can lead students to use other people's copyrighted work. However, filtering images for those that students can reuse helps. Go to images.google.com and do a search, then click "Tools" and "Usage Rights."

Take cell-phone photographs. This is one of the best ways to get custom images—perfect for what you need. Be the photographer and shoot your own photos! While teaching in a technology lab, educator Ken Shelton's students amassed a library of more than twelve thousand photos and more than one thousand hours of their own video footage. Students in Ken's classes added to that library and had constant access to it when creating their own work. Students' cell-phone cameras are, in most ways, as sharp and powerful as many digital cameras.

Use your webcam. Laptops, Chromebooks, and desktop computers typically come with a built-in webcam. Use it to your advantage! First, check whether your device has a camera app. If not, many programs and apps will connect to your webcam to take a picture. (Many of the G Suite tools, for example, let you insert an image with your webcam.)

Create custom graphics. Images don't have to be photos! Use a tool like Google Drawings (drawings.google.com), Canva (canva.com), or Adobe Spark (spark.adobe.com) to make your own graphics. Use shapes, lines, text, and other graphical elements to create useful, fun images! Download them as image files (.jpg or .png) to use in student work—or to teach with!

PICTURE-PERFECT LEARNING ACTIVITIES

We've seen that our brains were built to learn through images. We have some tools at our disposal: webcams, image searches, digital apps, whiteboards, even paper! So . . . what do we do with them? How can we create a learning experience with images?

Infographics. They're all over the place. You may have seen really long ones on Pinterest or social media. News outlets increasingly use them to share information. Infographics are an appealing, colorful blend of text and images designed to explain sometimes-complex ideas quickly and simply. If they're effective, brain-friendly, and fun, they can make amazing learning activities! It's definitely an experience to enjoy the process of making something—and being proud enough to share it with others afterward. Here's how to get started:

- Use a free digital tool like Google Drawings (drawings.google.com) or Canva (canva.com) to design them.
- Use snippets of text—short phrases, single sentences, or mini paragraphs.
- Back everything up with a visual—a graph, a picture, an icon from the Noun Project (thenounproject.com) or Flaticon (flaticon.com).
- Organize everything in a logical fashion—in segmented categories separated by lines, in a linear path with arrows, with numbered steps.
- Bring infographics to life with color! Color choices can help students organize and convey feelings and mood.

- Download infographics as image files. Create a shareable link. Add them to a class website or e-portfolio. Students can even share them on a class collaboration hub like Seesaw (web.seesaw.me). Remember the shared slides activity in the last chapter? You can have students download their infographic as an image and paste it on their own slide. Then students can collaborate, sharing comments about one another's slides!

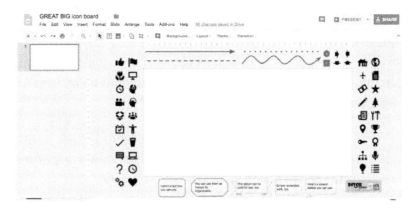

Save yourself—and your students—time in the infographics-creation process. Instead of having them start with a blank drawing, create a template for them in Google Slides or PowerPoint. Drop some icons, arrows, shapes, speech bubbles—anything they might use—in the space around the drawing. Ever notice that gray space around a digital document, slide, or drawing? It's actually your work space. It's like the space on your desk surrounding your laptop. If students find objects there to use in their infographics, they won't waste time looking for the *perfect* image. I have some precreated templates you can copy and use in Google Slides or PowerPoint. I call them icon boards because mine feature lots of icons! You can find them at DitchThatTextbook.com/iconboards.

Create your template and share it with students. You can use Google Classroom, attaching the template to an assignment and choosing "Make a copy for each student" from the drop-down menu. Or you can use the "Share" button to get a shareable link—anyone with the link can view. Then students can go to "File—Make a copy" and make their own copies.

Caption This! Images and speech/thought bubbles open up so many fun learning experiences! Missouri English teacher Laura Steinbrink and I wrote about these activities, calling them Caption This! We  love using Google Slides (slides.google.com) or Google Drawings (drawings.google.com) for these. You can use PowerPoint, too. To create your own:

- Get an image that relates to your content. Use an image search (Insert—Image—Search the Web). Take a picture with your webcam (Insert—Image—Camera).
- Draw in a speech/thought bubble (Insert—Shape—Callouts) to show what people in the image are likely thinking or saying.
- Label and identify any important parts of the image with an arrow shape (Insert—Shape—Arrows).
- Use a text box to justify your thinking, explaining why you think the characters would think or say that.

This activity is highly visual, it's fun, and it uses deeper thinking! It touches on three levels of Webb's Depth of Knowledge (2002), a measure of critical thinking. Students identify important elements of the image (level 1), take the perspective of the characters (level 2), and justify their decision (level 3). Plus, it's low-prep! If students can find their own images and draw in their own speech/thought bubbles and text boxes, it's virtually a no-prep activity. Everyone wins! See examples and more information about Caption This!

in this post I coauthored with Missouri educator Laura Steinbrink at DitchThatTextbook.com/captionthis.

Stop-motion animation.

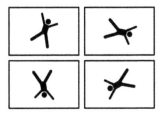

Without any fancy software or hardware, your students can create stop-motion animation. Just use Google Slides or PowerPoint, one of which your students likely already have access to. If students can envision an idea in motion, they can create it in motion with an animation! Go to DitchThatTextbook.com/stopmotion for detailed directions, but here's the basic idea:

- Create your first slide with everything on it to start the animation. If it's a story, this might include elements like characters, background, and setting. Example: if you're demonstrating mitosis (cell division), you'll need to draw out that original cell.
- Duplicate the first slide.
- Start your animation on that duplicated slide by moving items just a little bit in the direction they need to go.
- Duplicate the slide. Move those items some more. Duplicate and move. Duplicate and move. Repeat until your animation is complete!
- Put the slides in presentation mode. Flip through the slides with your arrow keys quickly to bring the animation to life!

Make your animations even more impressive by using some tips from tech-integration expert Jake Miller at DitchThatTextbook.com/stopmotiontips.

BookSnaps. In this activity, students first take a photo of a page in a book they're reading. Then, using any image-annotation tool (e.g., Seesaw, Google Slides/Drawings, PicCollage . . . even Snapchat!), students add their  thoughts and reflections. They can add emojis, Bitmojis, icons, et cetera . . . even draw on their #BookSnaps with their fingers. Then they turn them in, share them with the class—or share them with the world through a class website or social media! Go to DitchThatTextbook.com/booksnapsguide for video tutorials and examples by #BookSnaps creator Tara Martin.

Acrostic poems. These let students' personalities shine through! This idea, suggested by Texas educator Claudio Zavala, Jr., starts with the students' most personal detail—their  names. Then the students write a word to describe themselves that starts with each letter of their names, creating the form of a acrostic. They take self-portraits and add the acrostic poems to the images. Claudio suggests using Adobe Spark Post (spark.adobe.com), a free image-creation tool. You can see his instructions and an example at DitchThatTextbook.com/acrosticpoem.

Blackout poems. Author and artist Austin Kleon has popularized these and was my first introduction to them. Start with a page of text, like a newspaper or magazine article. You could even rip a page out of a textbook if you've ditched them! Find a handful of words  that make a clever, creative message related to what you're learning.

Black out all the other words using a marker, leaving just that clever message. You can do this with paper and markers. You can do it with Google Drawings, PowerPoint, or another image-annotation tool. For more details, go to DitchThatTextbook.com/blackoutpoetry.

Digital gallery walk. When students share work digitally, one characteristic seems to stand out: sitting. A lot of sitting. When sharing, viewing, and commenting, students are usually sitting down. Nationally, rising rates of obesity and type 2 diabetes are well documented, along with the harmful brain effects of too much sitting. How can we take a small step to get students out of their seats—and encourage them to share with an audience of their peers?

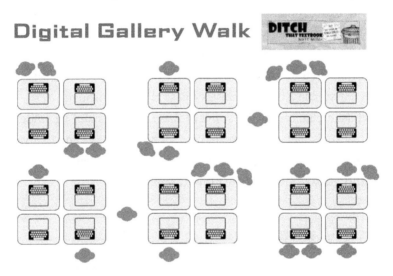

With the digital gallery walk, students display, share, and discuss work, much as if visiting an art museum. The activity goes like this:

- Students create an artifact of learning (like the activities in this chapter).
- When everyone is finished, students display their work on their screens.
- Students stand up and leave their devices on their desks.

- They circulate the room, stopping at their peers' desks (and devices) to check out their work.
- Students can also use the comment button in many apps/sites (especially G Suite) to leave feedback, like digital sticky notes.

Students get to move. They talk to one another face-to-face (seemingly a dying art!). It's a change of pace. Learn more about digital gallery walks at DitchThatTextbook.com/gallerywalk.

Finding the Visual Learning Hook

We want learning to be memorable. Sticky. Something students can take with them days, weeks, even years after class is over. Our brains love images. Students love seeing them, creating them, being in them. When we use them, students see themselves in the learning. Their personality, their interests—these all shine through.

Take a chance: try out some of these activities and let students create visuals. Better yet, dream up a highly visual activity that your students will love—because you know them best! You'll help them do work they're proud of, that they'll remember.

The Visual Hook

- How can we use the powerful blend of text and images to create buzzworthy shareable images for learning?
- How can we use our own sketching skills—even if they're very, very basic—to catch students' attention and bring a lesson to life? How can we empower our students to use those skills?

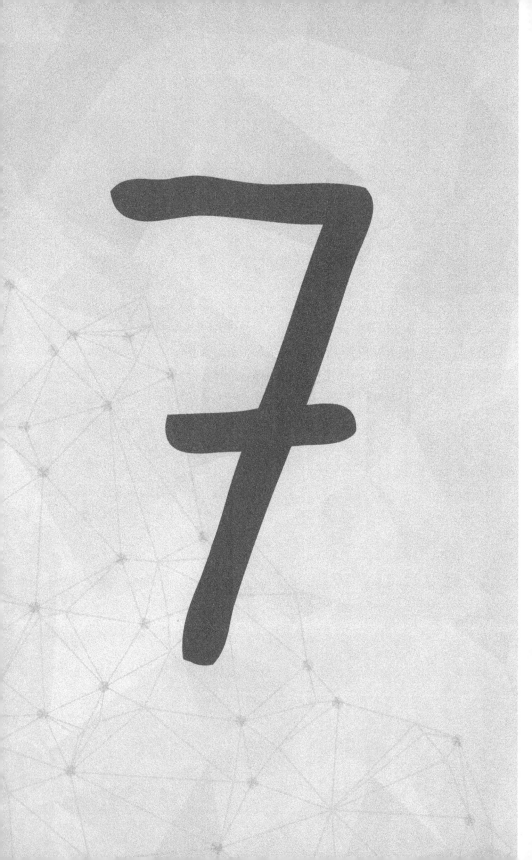

CHARTING THE COURSE TO A LEARNING EXPEDITION

In my years teaching in the classroom, I've been fortunate to work with some fantastic student explorers. Being an explorer is right at the heart of being a pirate! Pirates chart their own courses on the map. They sail the high seas. If they want to change course, they trim their sails and head in a different direction. The destination is up to them. When learning feels like this, students take the helm of the ship. Learning is a memorable experience because students own the learning.

I've had students who are geographical explorers, particularly after a video call with another class. I've hosted video calls with classes and guests all over the world, including Argentina, Australia, Canada, Singapore, and Spain. When my students had finished a video call with students in Europe, I asked them, "Do you want to see what their school and neighborhood look like?" I was met with an enthusiastic *yes,* which surprised me, because high school students aren't usually that excitable! We had *lots* of questions. What did the cars look like? How was their school similar to or different from ours? Using Google Maps Street View, we dropped ourselves down on the street right next to their school. The roads were tight. The cars were smaller. The trees were vastly different. The school grounds were smaller than ours and more tropical-looking. We had only visited their country on a projector screen in our classroom, and yet we came away feeling as if we'd visited another world—because, in many ways, we had! We understood our European virtual guests better than before and had a wider worldview. All in all, we were better and more inclusive global citizens than we had been when we started out.

I've had informational explorers, too. These students in my most advanced Spanish classes took some time to choose something they were passionate about. Then they set off to explore those topics by watching videos, listening to audio, and reading articles in Spanish wherever possible! When they came to a stopping point, they shared what they had learned—and what they already knew—with the class and with a bigger audience. One student was a skilled guitar player. He learned some key guitar vocabulary and created a YouTube channel full of tutorial videos in Spanish. Another student wanted to become an athletic trainer, so he created a website sharing tips and tricks for staying in shape and avoiding injury—also in Spanish! All projects were published to the web so anyone could find them. Lots of teachers and students are doing these projects during what they call Genius Hour. These explorers chart their own course based on their own interests. They create something they can be proud of and share with others. In the end, my students got to study something they loved using their Spanish that they wouldn't have studied on their own. I had my doubts and concerns at first. There were rocky moments where I worried we were way off the course we had charted. But in the end, we reached a destination that none of us could have imagined—and a result that thrilled us!

THREE TYPES OF EDUCATIONAL EXPLORERS

When students explore to learn, something magical happens. First, when they make decisions about what they'll learn, they make strides toward owning their education. That beats the "just do what the teacher tells you" model. Second, students pick subjects, topics, and processes that interest them. That means, as teachers, we don't have to guess what they're thinking! Finally, they learn in a way that sticks. Research shows that self-directed learning significantly enhances recognition memory (Markant et al. 2014). There are even gains when students have control of only the process, like pushing a button to advance to the next item. Bottom line: when students explore to learn, they can sail to new heights!

We'll cover three types of explorers that students become in PIRATE classrooms:

- Geographical explorers use rich map tools online to experience other worlds as if they're actually there. They pick up nuance and context—as well as pop culture and fun details!—they wouldn't encounter without going on that digital expedition.
- Informational explorers chart their own course to learning new content. They pick a topic—as broadly or tightly within the class topic of study as the teacher desires—and set sail. They don't know what they'll find when they begin, but that's half the adventure!
- Virtual explorers use the lands of virtual and augmented reality as their playgrounds. They manipulate and look closely at abstract ideas (e.g., the circulatory system) to make them more concrete. They create virtually, too, bringing their new ideas to a full, vibrant 3D life!

THE GEOGRAPHICAL EXPLORER

I've taught in a rural, sparsely populated county in Indiana. Many of my students have rarely left our county, let alone the state. There's so much of the world they haven't experienced. When your worldview is small, it's hard to understand what life is like for others. Sometimes, that worldview doesn't change until you set foot in another part of the world. During several short-term mission trips to Mexico City, I experienced the lifestyle, culture, poverty, and traffic of a world capital vastly different from my hometown.

For most of us, offering these life-changing experiences to students in-person isn't practical. But what if there were a way to

explore the world almost as if our sneakers were hitting the pavement of streets far across the globe? What if we could walk anywhere, observing every detail? Thankfully, there are ways to do just this with today's digital tools. It doesn't cost anything. You don't need an account. And you can display these far-off corners of the world on a projector or on digital devices for your students to see!

Tech Treasure Trove:
GEOGRAPHICAL EXPLORATION

- **Nearpod (nearpod.com)** virtual field trips let students travel the world through its hundreds of precreated virtual reality lessons. These trips aren't available through Nearpod's free plan, but if your school has purchased access, this is a great resource that's ready to go!
- Google Maps Treks **(google.com/maps/about/treks)** combine the panoramic views of Street View with multimedia, storytelling, and creativity. Connect the dozens of ready-made treks to your content for memorable, immersive learning.
- **Google Earth (earth.google.com)** calls itself "the world's most detailed globe." It primarily uses an aerial perspective but integrates well with Street View.
- **Google Tour Builder (tourbuilder.withgoogle.com)** lets you build stop-by-stop tours around the world, adding details to each location so viewers can read and learn.
- **Google Sky (google.com/sky)** lets you explore space and its stars, planets, and constellations—including close-up views of the moon, Mars, and other bodies in our solar system.

Digital exploration is an experience of inquiry in and of itself. Make it extra fun and memorable with just a few adjustments! Change the lighting in your room to match the location you're studying. (Gray paper over your windows would imitate Seattle. Pull the shades, turn off the overhead lights, and use selective lighting to simulate a space mission!) Move furniture and bring in different pieces to transform your classroom. (A French bistro is only a few high tables and stools away!)

Virtual walking tours, as described in Chapter 3, can become an experience if the students play the part! Dress up as the tour guide. Work on the accent. Include artifacts and props students can hold. Get more information at DitchThatTextbook.com/walkingtour.

THE INFORMATIONAL EXPLORER

When my students charted their own learning course through Genius Hour, I was only scratching the surface. When students make choices in what and how they learn, school is no longer something that's done *to* them. It's something they do on their own terms. Empowering students to be informational explorers can be as mild or as wild as you want.

Which of these questions would you like students to answer?

- How would you like to discuss this: digitally or with a partner?
- If we had to learn more about one part of this topic, what would it be?
- How can you show what you've learned? Record a video on Flipgrid? Make a stop-motion animation with Google Slides? Record a series of podcast episodes with Anchor?
- What aspect of this general subject would you like to study in greater depth?
- How would you design this course? What would you like to see covered? And what would you like to do?

Lots of great online resources help students follow their curiosity. Wonderopolis (wonderopolis.org) gives students a place to ask curiosity questions. (Why are flamingos pink? Why is Pluto no longer considered a planet? How do you make paper from a tree? How do roller coasters work?) The site helps students explore through video, images, explanations, resources, and challenges. *TweenTribune* (tweentribune.com) offers hundreds of current news articles, each available on a variety of lexile levels. It also offers self-scoring quizzes and critical thinking questions. Use these articles as a basis for lots of the creation ideas in this book—images, video, games, and more!

Chances are you have a fantastic resource already at your school to help students develop as informational explorers: your school librarian! Many are trained in library science and know just where to find what students are looking for. Consider starting with the library instead of a Google search. (Or start with a quick Google search and then go deeper by checking in with the librarian.)

Of course, not all online sources are equal. Media literacy is a crucial part of giving students the freedom to explore, helping them determine what is and isn't credible. Common Sense Media has some great media literacy resources.

THE VIRTUAL EXPLORER

We've already seen that exploring new worlds and new subjects is quite the experience. What about exploring virtual worlds—and creating virtual worlds of our own? Virtual reality and augmented reality are finding a place in the classroom. Students can have unforgettable, immersive experiences—and you don't even need any expensive virtual reality headsets! This part of the book is the most likely to go out-of-date quickly because augmented and virtual reality are new and rapidly developing technologies. Follow the #ARVRinEDU Twitter hashtag for discussions and ideas from practicing teachers. Classrooms are already being transformed by these exciting tools:

- **MERGE Cubes (mergeedu.com/cube)** let students hold and manipulate *anything* in augmented reality. How it works: Students hold a MERGE Cube, a specialized foam cube, and look at it through a device's camera using the MERGE app. On-screen, the app transforms the image of the cube into a globe, a shark, a dissected frog, a prism—the sky's the limit! By rotating the cube around, students can explore the object and examine it in greater detail. MERGE offers K–8 curriculum-aligned lessons with free and paid plans.

- **3DBear (3dbear.io)** turns students from virtual/augmented reality consumers into creators. Students can place objects in a virtual environment and tell stories with virtual reality. They can tap into creativity, critical thinking, social/emotional learning, and other higher-level skills.
- **Google Expeditions** is best known for hundreds of immersive virtual reality field trips. It also includes a library of dozens of augmented reality items to bring into the classroom, like a swirling tornado or a buzzing beehive. Though Expeditions is often used with virtual reality viewing kits, many of its features are available for free with mobile devices—even iPads, Chrome tablets, and touchscreen Chromebooks.

Finding the Exploration Hook

When you help students learn by exploring, they'll learn to pursue their passions and seize their futures. Exploration can be life-changing. It gives students permission to be curious, to dream, to wonder. And then to do something with their curiosity! The world is full of problems that call for big thinking—and even bigger solutions. It's important that students have every opportunity to explore this big world, to find their place in it and dream of the change they want to make. The framework and process can start in *your* classroom. Hand the learning over to your students. You'll teach them to craft the future!

The Exploration Hook

- How can we give students a choice in what they learn, to reflect their unique personalities and talents?
- Where can we take students digitally to let their curiosities run wild, sparking even more learning opportunities?

LEARNING WITH
NEW FRIENDS
AROUND
THE WORLD

Krista Harmsworth shared a beautiful dream with her childhood friend Sue Anne Prazak. When they were girls, they planned to raise their kids together when they grew up. They'd live on the same street in their home state of Arizona and teach at the same school. They were both going to be teachers, and they were going to do it together.

When they grew up, their plans changed. Krista moved to a suburb of Detroit, Michigan, and Sue Anne stayed in Arizona. They both did become teachers. They weren't physical neighbors, but they got to be virtual classroom neighbors. They decided that Krista's students and Sue Anne's students—all fifth graders—could learn a lot from each other even if they lived two thousand miles apart.

Krista and Sue Anne set up a Google Hangouts video call. As soon as they laid eyes on the other class, the Arizona kids marveled at the Michigan kids' heavy sweaters. The Michigan kids noticed the Arizona kids' tank tops. When the Michigan students shared the first snowfall of the year with Arizona kids who had never seen snow, it was even more special. The two classes shared photos and favorite foods in a Google Slides presentation—a kind of yearbook just for them. This was an experience!

When both classes read *The City of Ember* by Jeanne DuPrau, Krista and Sue Anne achieved a version of their childhood dream. They taught together in the same room virtually through Google Hangouts. The teachers took turns reading aloud to both classes during the video calls. They used common language, discussing figurative language and using signposts. It was as if they were a reading-and-language-arts team in the same building. They created an Edmodo online classroom. Students could discuss the book virtually there at any time. Small virtual discussion groups brought their findings to the class video call later in the week.

"In Michigan, the whole idea of connecting that far away was barely being touched," Krista says. "This was kind of a big thing."

But then Krista and Sue Anne took it to another level.

Krista flew home to Arizona for Christmas. She stayed there through the first day of school for the new semester. Krista walked into Sue Anne's classroom and pretended to be her sub. Wrote her name on the board: *Mrs. Harmsworth*. It took the Arizona kids a moment, but they got it. "Hey, you're Mrs. Harmsworth! Wait . . . you're from Michigan. How is this happening?"

Back in Krista's class in Michigan, the substitute teacher was playing along, too. "Mrs. Harmsworth doesn't want to fall behind in her lesson plans," the sub told the students. "That means we can't miss this video call with the class in Arizona." The call started, and then it was time for Krista's Michigan kids to get a surprise. Krista popped onto the screen—in Arizona! Her students were stunned.

The whole connected classroom experience, start to finish, was incredibly worthwhile, Krista says.

"That's something ten-year-olds struggle with: knowing that there's more out there," she says. "They're not as aware about the outside world. They're just starting to learn about it. Whether you're in Michigan or Arizona, ten-year-olds are ten-year-olds. There is a bigger world out there—not just our school and our community. It takes people from everywhere to make the world go round."

It was a memorable year for those students. Will the Michigan students remember those kids they met from Arizona? Will the Arizona students remember when the teacher from Michigan actually came to their class? I think it's a safe bet!

That classroom connection was memorable because it touched the kids emotionally. A strong emotional response inscribes learning experiences in memory for years to come.

"Emotional learning has a strong influence on memory formation and its long-term consolidation," writes Sanchari Sinha Dutta, PhD, on the News Medical website (2018). "Consolidation is considered a slow process, during which the memories are not yet considered permanently set. This might allow opportunity for an emotional reaction related to an event to influence its storage and increase the likelihood of it being remembered."

Memorable experience. Sticky learning. It works, and not just because of the technology. The students weren't excited about Google Hangouts. It's not the app. It's the human connection. Help students learn from people who inspire them, and the learning may last a lifetime.

Video calls, social media, and the like are very much mainstream these days. FaceTime calls to a friend, Facebook comments, and pictures on Snapchat are not uncommon. But taking these interactions into the classroom for learning—on safe, education-centric platforms—makes you an outlier.

Will teachers create these learning experiences with video calls and digital connections? Often, it isn't a matter of access. It's a matter of intention. We must decide to try it because it has promise. It has potential for fantastic, long-lasting lessons.

It's a matter of *iteration*. Try something. Reinforce what goes well. Learn from and reconfigure the things that don't go well at first. But it's also a matter of *inspiration*—finding a way, somehow, to spark passion in your students.

Tech Treasure Trove:
DIGITAL COLLABORATION ON THE CHEAP

You probably have the tools. At the bare minimum, you need a laptop, Chromebook, iPad, something connected to the internet. You can display the call to your whole class. If your students have access to devices (a lab, a cart of devices, a one-device-to-one-student environment), here are a few ways you can take it to the next level.

Video calls. Platforms like Skype, FaceTime, and Google Hangouts Meet can give your students a face-to-face connection with people, places, and experiences around the world. Connect with another class. Visit a location virtually. Hear from a guest speaker. *Activities can include talking with a guest speaker, working with a partner classroom, or taking a virtual field trip.*

Creation tools. So many elements of G Suite (Docs, Slides, Sheets, Drawings, Sites, etc.) offer options for real-time collaboration. Use the "Share" button and create a shareable link with the "Anyone can edit" option. Students can write in a document together or design slides

together. Many other web tools allow for online collaboration. Look for terms like *collaborators* and *edit* as clues that this feature exists. Then test it out to see how it works. *Activities can include asking/ answering questions in a shared document, building slide decks together to demonstrate understanding, or doing many of the activities mentioned in previous chapters of this book together.*

Online hubs. These feel like social media for the classroom but are created specifically for academic collaboration. Platforms like Seesaw (web.seesaw.me), Edmodo (edmodo.com), Google Classroom (classroom.google.com), and Canvas (canvaslms.com) each provide a centralized location for sharing, discussing,

and working. *Activities can include taking quick polls, engaging in Q&A or discussions, or posting student work and commenting on it.*

MAKING THE CLASSROOM CONNECTION

Integral to creating a collaborative experience is finding the right partners. The success of your experiences will depend on the people you put in front of your students. Who will you connect with? How do you find them? Often, teachers who want to try this get discouraged by the question of identifying virtual guests. It's simpler than you may think. Here are some ideas:

- **Find the right person and just ask.** It's amazing how far a simple Google search can go. I wrote in *Ditch That Homework* (2015) about my friend Todd Shriver. He teaches a social studies class called History of the '80s. He scheduled amazing virtual guests for his class—like Malcolm-Jamal Warner from *The Cosby Show* and US Olympic hockey legend Mike Eruzione—just by asking.
- **Ask your colleagues, family, and friends for ideas.** You might be surprised at who you have a connection to through the people you already know. A simple question in the school hallway or on social media can reveal a wealth of options.
- **Search the Microsoft Educator Community.** This database (at SkypeInTheClassroom.com) has hundreds of virtual guests, dozens of virtual field trips, and thousands of teachers and classes. It's free to search and free to use.
- **Access databases through other platforms.** Lots of organizations and companies help make connections for you. Flipgrid (flipgrid.com), the video communication tool, has established "GridPals," like a video pen pal service. The mission of Empatico (empatico.org) is to connect classrooms around the world. Nepris (nepris.com) makes connections between education and industry.

- **Leverage social media.** If you know where to look, social media can be a rich resource for finding collaboration partners. Kansas educator and Skype Master Teacher Dyane Smokorowski suggests this tip. Do this Google search: "site:twitter.com ornithologist," but replace "ornithologist" with a description of the kind of person you want to connect with. If you find people who are active on Twitter, there's a good chance they will be responsive to a request to collaborate with your class.

MAKING COLLABORATION AN EXPERIENCE

Making a personal connection with people around the country—or the globe—is often a memorable experience in and of itself. But how can we turn up the wow factor, create some classroom fireworks that will get students talking? Consider adding some of these elements to your video calls or collaborations:

- **FedEx days:** Giving students a problem to solve is a fantastic way to apply learning in many situations. It can be a great way to demonstrate learning and transfer it in a real-life context. The design-thinking process can be a very useful framework. As part of the problem-solving process, ask students to prototype their ideas. Take a cue from the Craft Store Hook in *Teach Like a PIRATE* (Burgess 2012). Pipe cleaners. Toilet-paper rolls. Straws. Hot glue. Cardboard—lots and lots of cardboard! Have students deliver a prototype in one day. In the business world,

this kind of activity has been called a "FedEx day" because FedEx delivers packages in one day! Students present their creations to a partner class on a video call. Or in a twist on the show *Shark Tank*, invite a business leader or expert to view student pitches and provide feedback!

- **All the Skype's a stage:** Elements of theater aren't just for in-class skits. When presenting an idea, a story, or anything to a partner on a video call, act it out! Change the lighting. Dress someone up to play a part. Build props or scenery using cardboard, existing classroom furniture, and bulletin board paper. Props and puppets can give a call a new dimension. Creating and playing recurring characters can be fun, too. When they pop up again, students recognize them!

- **Collaborative music:** With digital music-creation tools like Soundtrap (soundtrap.com), TwistedWave (twistedwave.com), and Audacity (audacityteam.org), students from another state—or country!—can create music and other recordings and mix them together for a finished

product. Use a metronome or other method of making sure you're all playing/singing/performing in time. Or record audio clips and cut/paste them together. Think of the result: a recorded masterpiece created from locations scattered across the map!

- **Mystery Skype:** This one's been around for a while, but it never fails to create an experience! Mystery Skype is a global guessing game where classes join on a video call and try to guess each other's location. Often, classes ask yes/no questions of each other, slowly narrowing down the geographic location until they can guess. If geographical guessing isn't your thing, there are alternate games: Mystery Animal Skype, Mystery Number Skype, Mystery

Instrument Skype, and so on. You can always make up your own alternate game! Find more Mystery Skype resources at DitchThatTextbook.com/mysteryskype.

- **Escape rooms:** The goal of an escape room: find clues, interpret the clues, find a way out of the room. Education has seen a fun twist on these in Breakout EDU, which uses "breakout boxes" instead of locked rooms. Partner with another class on a video call. Get a breakout box in each room (by buying them, building them, or making a suitable version of them). Each class has the same clues (which can tie into content you're currently learning). Then it's a race! Who can break out first?

- **Pop culture:** What's popular where your partner class is located? In your location? In the United States, student obsessions have run the gamut. The Harlem Shake. Fidget spinners. The floss dance. Video games. Fashion. Food. When students share each other's passions or latest trends, it can be a fun bonding experience—and provide insight into another culture!

- **Long-distance Kahoot!:** Your students may have played Kahoot! (kahoot.com), a game show–style review game. But have they played it with students from another state or country? Get on a video call with another class and start a

How to set up a distance Kahoot!/Quizizz game

| Create a Kahoot! / Quizizz game (or choose one to use). | Start a whole group video call with the other class. | Students in both classes log on to their devices and go to the join game page. | Project the web page with ?s or progress to your class AND share that screen with the other class. | Run the game as normal -- but to both classes instead of just one! |

Kahoot! game. Project the screen with the questions to your students and share that screen with the other class through the video call. Both classes play the game at once! This works for other games, too, like Quizizz (quizizz.com) and Quizlet Live (quizlet.com).

- **New endings, new friends:** You've studied a story, a historical happening, or something in current events. Your students know the details. Now imagine: what would happen if the story ended differently? How would life have changed? How would the world have been different? Students from your class and a partner class can collaborate to create these Choose Your Own Adventure–type stories together. They can create in Google Slides, sharing the file with each other, and giving "anyone with the link can edit" access. Find how-to instructions for this activity at DitchThatTextbook.com/newendings.

Finding the Human Connections Hook

Connections are powerful. They can help us do more, become more.

For me, getting connected on social media (Twitter, specifically) changed my teaching career. In fact, it *saved* my teaching career. The people, the ideas, the encouragement—all of them pulled me out of a rut that was killing my career. Twitter—and all that I found there—reinvigorated the sense of my calling to education.

For Krista Harmsworth and Sue Anne Prazak, it was calling on their own personal strengths in teaching and joining them together. They created an experience—one they couldn't have quite duplicated otherwise—by introducing their students, who learned both about and from one another.

There's a wise piece of advice, possibly an old African proverb: "If you want to go fast, go alone. If you want to go far, go together."

We're better together. It's truer in today's world than ever before. We can accomplish more. Brainstorm better ideas. Support and encourage one another. And when we work together to make a difference in this world, to push for change, the world is a better place because of it. In *Teach Like a PIRATE* (2012), Dave Burgess calls this the "life-changing lesson."

If our idea of collaboration in class goes no farther than "think, pair, share," we're missing a phenomenal opportunity to teach and learn. To make the world seem a little less vast. To make a difference and change someone's life. It might be our students' lives. It might be our own.

The Human Connections Hook

- How can we pair with another class so that each class learns from the other and we expand our possibilities? Can we do a video call, collaborate on a digital file, plan an initiative together?
- Who can we pull into our class digitally to enrich the conversation and provide a unique perspective on what we're learning?
- Where can we go virtually that helps students understand a topic—and the world as a whole—a little better?

If our idea of collaboration in class goes no farther than "think, pair, share," we're missing a phenomenal opportunity to teach and learn.

SLAYING
DOUBT AND
ROADBLOCKS

Ready to tech like a PIRATE? I have some news for you. Consider this your warning.

It's not going to be easy.

Lots of roadblocks will stand in your way. Technology will fail on you. Lessons will blow up in your face. People might not understand what you're trying to accomplish. The toughest doubter of all might be you yourself.

I feel you. You're not alone. But I often come back to this line from Dave Burgess: "It's not supposed to be easy. It's supposed to be worth it."

We may know it's worth it. But when things get hard, we need a little encouragement. We need some reassurance that we're on the right path. That the fight is worth fighting.

In this chapter, I've written you some letters of encouragement. You can tuck them away for just the right moment, or you can go ahead and read them now. You're moving in the right direction. You're going to be all right. Let me show you what I mean.

DOUBT

I can totally sympathize with this. If it makes you feel any better, I still have doubts. I still get overwhelmed. Sometimes, doubt paralyzes me and I stop. The truth is that everyone feels this way. You're not alone, and your experience isn't unusual.

Let's break this down piece by piece. First, the doubt. When I started trying new ideas in my class, no one gave me permission. The truth is that you don't need permission from anyone to do your best teaching. Disagree? OK, let's try this. I, Matt Miller, the author of this book, hereby give you permission to try new ideas that you truly believe will help you to do your best teaching. Is that what you needed? If so, you got it.

Once you get started, you may start to feel something I felt a *lot*: imposter syndrome. It's the feeling that you're a fraud and that everyone is going to figure that out and expose you for it. When I was teaching every day, I felt this on a *very* regular basis. Now that I work with teachers and write and create for a living, I feel it even more often.

The truth is that your students *need* you. Those students are silently begging you to do your very best teaching. They don't care if it doesn't look like anyone else's in your hallway, your school, or even your local area. You be you. Give it your best shot. If it doesn't work out the way you hoped, there's always tomorrow . . . and I'll bet your students will be more forgiving than you can imagine.

OVERWHELM

I'M OVERWHELMED. THERE ARE SO MANY IDEAS, OPTIONS, POSSIBILITIES, DIGITAL TOOLS, STRATEGIES, AND ON AND ON. I FEEL LIKE I DON'T KNOW WHAT I DON'T KNOW. I DON'T EVEN KNOW WHERE TO START – OR IF I SHOULD START.

I heard a really good explanation of the "overwhelm" feeling once. I think that it will empower you and set you free. Feeling overwhelmed isn't the problem of having too many options. It's not knowing where to start. It's like that old saying. The journey of a thousand miles begins with a single step.

You're right. There are *so* many ideas, options, possibilities, digital tools, and strategies. Every single day there are more. That doesn't mean you have to use them all. You aren't required to know about all of them. I don't know about all of them. Neither of us has to. All you really need is what's going to get the job done for you and your students.

Overwhelm is the problem of not knowing where to start. So where do you start? I have three suggestions for you:

1. **Start small.** Find one lesson. One part of one lesson. Maybe it's one of those "It can't get any worse than this!" lessons. Do you have any of those? (Let's be honest—*everyone* has some of those!) If it makes you think *I can do that!* you've chosen wisely.

2. **Start with impact.** What area can have the biggest potential impact on your students? Start there. Don't worry about getting the answer wrong here. There are probably lots of possibilities for great impact. Base your choice on what you'd like to see improve first.

3. **Start with excitement.** What are you excited about? My wife and I have a rule about cleaning the house: never mess with motivation. If we get motivated to clean late at night, early in the morning, or at any other inconvenient time, we just roll with it. Don't mess with your motivation. It will sustain your new ideas.

You *can* beat that overwhelm if you start small, start with impact, and start with excitement. You can do this.

CREATIVITY

> I'M NOT CREATIVE. I'M NOT AN ARTIST. I DON'T MAKE MUSIC. I'M NOT ONE OF THOSE CREATIVE TYPES, AND ALL OF THESE CREATIVE IDEAS ARE JUST NOT FOR ME.

There are *lots* of teachers—and people in all walks of life—who feel the same as you. Whenever you say you're not creative, you're assigning yourself a label. *Not creative.* Over time, I'll bet you let that label form your identity. Changing your identity is hard work.

You don't need the "creative" label to do creative work. I think of creativity as a muscle. It's something that anyone can use at any point. But the more that you develop it, the stronger it gets.

Think of it this way: I'm from Indiana, where basketball is very popular. Some of the best scorers in the NBA display their creativity in the innovative ways they get to the basket and score when it seems impossible. They dribble around defenders, slash to the basket, and contort their bodies to get the shot off. We're left thinking, *I would have never been able to do that!* How do they develop that creativity? They develop their ball-handling skills with drills. They play in live games. They watch others, absorbing their moves and adding them to their repertoire. Then, in a game, they see an opening to the basket that they wouldn't have been able to otherwise because now they've developed that creative vision.

Start by making some small creative choices. (Include a couple small pop culture references in your class.) Start with what feels comfortable. (Start illustrating on the board a bit more if you're comfortable with art.) Start with what is exciting. (Include a new video option for students if your students talk about their favorite YouTubers.) Then, like a skilled basketball player, adjust on your way to the hoop. When you commit to developing your skills little by little, you'll be surprised at how quickly those creative capacities improve.

TECHINESS

I'll let you in on a little secret, something to you from me, a person who feels like he's somewhat techy. I'm not a technology superstar, though, and I dedicate much of my professional life to helping teachers use technology in their classes! I'm not on the cutting, bleeding edge. And I can't keep up with all the new apps and digital tools and all the latest features.

The truth is that you don't have to. Your students don't need you to. Your school doesn't need you to. Now that you've read that, breathe a sigh of relief.

If you've been teaching for any amount of time, you probably have something that works—a method for teaching reading, a trick for remembering vocabulary, a successful way of using a particular app. (Even if it doesn't work as well as you'd hope, it works.) That's your baseline. Now let's find a way to make it better when you tech like a PIRATE:

- **Brainstorm.** Think of what you want students to accomplish and what digital tools you have at your disposal.
- **Use a critical eye.** When you have an idea of how technology could support teaching and learning, ask yourself: *Does the technology make the lesson better in some way?* Sometimes you have to give it a try before you know.
- **Reflect.** The first time you try something new, it might not go as well as you'd hoped. It might feel like a colossal failure. Try not to let your default response to failure be *I'll never do that again.* Try to figure out why it didn't work and find a new path to take next time.
- **Watch.** Keep an eye out for new ideas to try. Twitter is my pipeline for new ideas. I love keeping up with how educators use technology in innovative ways in their classrooms. I also use Twitter to see what new features and new digital tools are available. Want to get started? Check out the free *A Beginner's Guide to Twitter for Educators* e-book available at DitchThatTextbook.com/twitterebook.

If you feel like you're less than enough because you don't know all the technology tools and tricks, don't worry. None of us do. Find what you need to do what you need to.

MOMENTUM

I LOST MY MOMENTUM. I STARTED STRONG, BUT I'VE HIT A SETBACK. I CAN'T SEEM TO GET GOING AGAIN. I THINK IF I COULD HIT MY STRIDE, I'D BE FINE.

I've been through this so many times myself. In fact, in the writing of this book, I've lost my momentum several times and have wondered if I'd ever finish. In the classroom, I've sat at my desk, thinking, *I don't even know what to do next. I don't even want to do anything next.*

Jon Acuff (2017) describes the antidote for motivation malaise in his book *Finish,* which is all about completing your goals. It all has to do with the "day after perfect." When you want to accomplish something, the default thinking says that the most important day is the first day. "The journey of a thousand miles begins with a single step," someone might tell you. "The first step is your biggest obstacle." Wrong. According to Acuff, taking the first step is much easier than dealing with the "day after perfect." The "day after perfect" comes when you hit a snag. Your perfect streak of days without a mistake comes to an end. That's the dangerous moment, Acuff says. That's when you lose your momentum and the whole thing can grind to a halt. It can bring an end to your best-laid plans.

You say you've lost your momentum? Consider today the "day after perfect," even if your official "day after perfect" was weeks, months, or even years ago. Today's the day to start a new streak. Acknowledge your situation. Repeat after me: "I hit a bump in the road. But what I'm building is too important. I'll start a new streak right now."

You can. And you will. You can do this.

RESISTANCE

Maybe what you're trying to change is bigger than you realize. And maybe, just maybe, if you realize what you're really trying to do, you'll find the encouragement to keep doing it.

When you try new ideas in your classroom, you're not just changing your teaching. You're changing the culture in your classroom. You might not realize it, but in small, persistent ways, you're nudging the culture in your entire school. (I know. That's big. But don't let that scare you. Lean into it. Let me explain.)

Students get comfortable with the way that school is done. You may have heard the "game of school" analogy. Kids learn how the game is played (grading, discipline, student-teacher relationships). They learn how they can win at it (collecting points, following rules, compliance). When you start changing the rules, the players of the game get unsettled. They have to come up with new strategies. They learn how to play the new version of the game. This is what happens when you break away from the traditional ways of teaching that aren't serving students and try something new. You're shifting the culture of your classroom. You'll feel it with your students. There's a chance you'll even feel it in other places. Maybe you'll hear other teachers talking about you. Maybe you'll get parent phone calls—or your principal will get them. Those are the effects of the nudge you're making to your entire school's culture. Whether you set out to do it or not, you're doing it.

Culture isn't changed overnight. But persistent effort over time will pay off. Think of it like trying to move a boulder. Pursuing your new ideas is like persistently pushing on the boulder. You're pushing and pushing, but that boulder just won't budge. After pushing for a while, you start to wonder if the boulder will ever move. You think, *Am I the crazy fool who will never learn and keeps pushing an immovable object?*

Suddenly, that boulder moves. It budges ever so slightly forward. You keep applying pressure, and the budge becomes a roll. Finally, the boulder is rolling forward, and your persistence helps it keep picking up speed.

Many times, we want to quit pushing that boulder right before it starts to budge. You'll never know if that budge is right around the corner or not. But if the change is worth making, maybe you keep pushing on that boulder. (Notice that I said *maybe*. Some boulders are harder to move than others. The culture in some places will take a long, long time to change. In that case, you have a decision to make: do you persistently keep pushing that same boulder, or do you find a new boulder to push?)

I wrote those letters just for you, and I hope you feel better about yourself and the important work you're doing. Repeat after me:

- My work with my students is important.
- I want to do my best for them.
- I want to be at my best for them.
- When I find something that's not best for them, I'm brave enough to make a change.
- I am a highly qualified professional who is dedicated to serving my students.
- To prepare them for the future, I can't always rely on what we've done in the past.
- I realize that it may not be easy or smooth at the beginning.
- I'm willing to be brave and accept that.
- I will let Maya Angelou's quote guide me: "I did then what I knew how to do. Now that I know better, I do better."

You can do this!

AFTERWORD

TAKE THE MAVERICK TEACHER CREED

Back in the Introduction, I talked about Maverick, the gutsy fighter pilot in the movie *Top Gun*. Maverick takes some risks and breaks tradition, but he does so when the potential rewards are too great to ignore. Starting now, let's commit to being maverick teachers:

1. Maverick teachers identify ineffective activities, lessons, and teaching practices.

2. Maverick teachers commit to finding better ways to teach—even if they don't know what that looks like yet.

3. Maverick teachers brainstorm new ideas in a nonjudgmental way (because more ideas lead to better ideas).

4. Maverick teachers make the best plans they can based on the best wisdom they have at the time.

5. Maverick teachers bravely try their best to create learning experiences that make a positive difference in their students' lives.

6. Maverick teachers evaluate their efforts honestly and critically to find ways to improve—and they take action to improve.

7. Maverick teachers refuse to dwell on failure, and constantly find ways to do better the next time.

Do you believe in the maverick teacher creed? Want to take the maverick teacher pledge? Go to DitchThatTextbook.com/maverickpledge. Create your certificate. Sign it and hang it where you'll see it when you teach. Classrooms everywhere will be stronger and more memorable when we unleash a community of maverick teachers!

Remember, you don't have to do this alone, either. If you have like-minded maverick colleagues in your school or nearby, you're fortunate. You can create your own creative teaching collaborative, a little troupe of changemakers. You might be surprised at how far the effects may reach. These collaboratives already exist online. If the ideas in this book have resonated with you, I'll suggest two places to connect on Twitter:

- **Search for #ditchbook.** With this hashtag, teachers collaborate about how to ditch textbooks and textbook traditions, based on the ideas in my first book, *Ditch That Textbook* (2015). Those of us who use this hashtag talk about how to use tech in meaningful ways and how to teach in light of the techy world we live in.
- **Search for #tlap, which stands for *Teach Like a PIRATE*.** It's all about creating a learning experience instead of just teaching a lesson. (And if we use tech to do that, #tlap could also stand for the title of this book, *Tech Like a PIRATE*!) You'll see teachers sharing what they're doing to make class memorable and engaging with this hashtag.

As you search these and find other educators on Twitter, you'll find other hashtags. Many of these represent powerful communities of educators. They share ideas. They discuss strategy. They dream of a better education world. They're there to encourage, challenge, lift up, and support. Leaning on other educators for ideas and encouragement isn't a weakness. For me, it's been a vital part of my growth and learning as an educator.

Social media—and those we meet there—can help us with ideas. They can provide us with a spark. But that only takes us so far. Then, it's time to *do* something. I've seen a phenomenon in myself, and then I noticed it in other educators. We often use education talk and ideas—blog posts, social media, podcasts, books—as entertainment rather than a call to action. We read and read and read. Tweet and tweet and tweet. Then we don't do anything with it. Avoid that trap! Read, listen, consume only as much as you need to make change. Then, go out and do something with it! Those amazing ideas can't change the lives of students if we don't put them into practice.

You'll find a treasure trove of additional resources related to the ideas in this book at DitchThatTextbook.com/TechLAP.

Don't just teach a lesson. Create an experience! I hope you've seen enough research and anecdotes throughout this book to know that this idea isn't just fluff. Turning learning into an experience—mentally, emotionally, through the senses—can create long-lasting memory. It can help students make connections to content that stick with them throughout their lives. And it can spark passion! In Chapter 4, I mentioned gaming expert Jane McGonigal. I met her when she gave a keynote speech at a conference. She signed my copy of her book *SuperBetter*. On the title page she wrote, "Play with purpose!" I've learned more and more over time how important a goal that is. Play is a force, and it can actually help us meet our goals—with lots of smiles along the way!

Plutarch wrote centuries ago that education was not the filling of a pail, but rather, the lighting of a fire. I think that's a perfect description of this book's message. With a fire, your job is just to light it. Maybe tend it a bit as it grows. But once the first spark is ignited, it roars to a blaze—on its own. Once it roars, it's unstoppable. It burns bright no matter what we do. Transferring knowledge to students takes them only so far. But when we help them light a roaring fire of passion, that's when futures are changed and lives are impacted.

Pirates and technology. Who would've guessed? Use your hooks. Sail the seven seas of engagement. Keep the treasure map handy, and use your compass to make sure you're headed in the right direction. This is a voyage your students—and *you*—are going to love!

SUPER

BETTER

For Matt,

A Revolutionary
Approach to Getting
Stronger, Happier,
Braver, *and*
More Resilient*

play with purpox!!

Jane McGonigal

*POWERED BY THE SCIENCE OF GAMES

REFERENCES

Achor, Shawn. 2011. *The Happiness Advantage: The Seven Principles That Fuel Success and Performance at Work*. London: Virgin.

Acuff, Jon. 2017. *Finish: Give Yourself the Gift of Done*. New York: Portfolio/Penguin.

Braff, Danielle. 2011. "Movies May Cause Special Effects on the Body." *Chicago Tribune*, June 22, 2011. chicagotribune.com/lifestyles/ct-xpm-2011-06-22-sc-health-0622-movies-impact-on-body-20110622-story.html.

Burgess, Dave. 2012. *Teach Like a PIRATE: Increase Student Engagement, Boost Your Creativity, and Transform Your Life as an Educator*. San Diego, CA: Dave Burgess Consulting.

Cisco Public. 2019. White paper. "Cisco Visual Networking Index: Forecast and Trends, 2017–2022 ." Cisco. February 27, 2019. cisco.com/c/en/us/solutions/collateral/service-provider/visual-networking-index-vni/complete-white-paper-c11-481360.html.

Csikszentmihalyi, Mihaly. 1997. *Finding Flow: The Psychology of Engagement with Everyday Life*. New York: Basic Books.

Dutta, Sanchari Sinha. 2018. "The Limbic System and Long-Term Memory." *News Medical*. August 23, 2018. news-medical.net/health/The-Limbic-System-and-Long-Term-Memory.aspx.

Edison Research. 2020. "The Infinite Dial®." Edison Research, March 20, 2020. edisonresearch.com/the-infinite-dial/.

Enberg, Jasmine. 2018. "Hey Alexa, Who's Using Smart Speakers? eMarketer's Forecast for 2018." May 29, 2018. emarketer.com/content/hey-alexa-whos-using-smart-speakers.

García, Emma, and Elaine Weiss. 2019. "The Teacher Shortage Is Real, Large and Growing, and Worse than We Thought: The First Report in 'The Perfect Storm in the Teacher Labor Market' Series." Economic Policy Institute. March 26, 2019. epi.org/publication/the-teacher-shortage-is-real-large-and-growing-and-worse-than-we-thought-the-first-report-in-the-perfect-storm-in-the-teacher-labor-market-series/.

Hammond, Zaretta. 2015. *Culturally Responsive Teaching and the Brain: Promoting Authentic Engagement and Rigor among Culturally and Linguistically Diverse Students.* Thousand Oaks, CA.

Hasson, Uri, Yuval Nir, Ifat Levy, Galit Fuhrmann, and Rafael Malach. 2004. "Intersubject Synchronization of Cortical Activity during Natural Vision." *Science* 303, no. 5664 (2004): 1634–40.

Just, Marcel, and Melissa Ludtke. 2010. "Watching the Human Brain Process Information." Nieman Reports. June 29, 2010. niemanreports.org/articles/watching-the-human-brain-process-information/.

Kleon, Austin. 2012. *Steal Like an Artist. Steal Like an Artist: 10 Things Nobody Told You about Being Creative.* New York: Workman Publishing.

LaBar, K. S., and Cabeza, R. 2006. "Cognitive Neuroscience of Emotional Memory." *Nature Reviews Neuroscience* 7, no. 1 (2006): 54.

Markant, Douglas, Sarah DuBrow, Lila Davachi, and Todd M. Gureckis. 2014. "Deconstructing the Effect of Self-Directed Study on Episodic Memory." *Memory & Cognition* 42, no. 8 (2014): 1211–24.

Matera, Michael. 2015. *Explore Like a Pirate: Engage, Enrich, and Elevate Your Learners with Gamification and Game-Inspired Course Design.* San Diego, CA: Dave Burgess Consulting.

McGonigal, Jane. 2016. *SuperBetter: The Power of Living Gamefully.* New York: Penguin USA.

McGonigal, Jane. 2020. "Our Story Starts with Jane." SuperBetter. Accessed March 22, 2020. superbetter.com/about.

Miller, Matt. 2015. *Ditch That Textbook: Free Your Teaching and Revolutionize Your Classroom.* San Diego: Dave Burgess Consulting.

Miller, Matt, and Alice Keeler. 2017. *Ditch That Homework: Practical Strategies to Help Make Homework Obsolete.* San Diego, CA: Dave Burgess Consulting, Incorporated.

Miller, Michael, C. Mangano, Y. Park, R. Goel, G. D. Plotnick, and R. A. Vogel. 2006. "Impact of Cinematic Viewing on Endothelial Function." *Heart* 92, no. 2 (2006): 261–2.

National Association of Colleges and Employers. 2019. "Job Outlook 2020." National Association of Colleges and Employers, November 2019. naceweb.org/store/2019/job-outlook-2020/.

National Institute for Play. The Opportunities. "Education." No date. nifplay.org/opportunities/education/.

The Nielsen Company. 2017. "Mobile Kids: The Parent, the Child and the Smartphone." February 28, 2017. nielsen.com/us/en/insights/article/2017/mobile-kids-the-parent-the-child-and-the-smartphone/.

Wikipedia. 2020. "Talk Page Guidelines." Wikimedia Foundation, March 20, 2020. en.wikipedia.org/wiki/Wikipedia:Talk_page_guidelines.

Webb, Norman L. 2002. "Depth-of-knowledge levels for four content areas." *Language Arts* 28, no. March (2002).

Weinberger, David. 2011. *Too Big to Know: Rethinking Knowledge Now That the Facts Aren't the Facts, Experts Are Everywhere, and the Smartest Person in the Room Is the Room.* New York: Basic Books, 2011.

Zomorodi, Manoush, host. 2016. "The Secret to Making Video Games Good for You." September 21, 2016. Note To Self (podcast). wnycstudios.org/story/video-games-wellness-depression.

ACKNOWLEDGMENTS

I'm grateful to my professional learning network online. You saved me from the despair of an uninspired classroom when I wanted to quit education. You've given me new teaching ideas. You've challenged my assumptions. You've inspired and encouraged me when I needed it most. If you've written a tweet I saw, thank you. If you've read or replied to one of my tweets, thank you. If you've touched my life—or other educators' lives—through social media, thank you.

The team supporting Dave Burgess Consulting (Dave and Shelley Burgess, Wendy Van Dyk, Tara Martin, Sal Borriello, and others) have encouraged my work. They've made my writing sound like a better version of myself. They've infused life and excitement into countless classrooms across the globe, affecting thousands and thousands of children. Thank you.

My wife, Melanie, is my biggest cheerleader and pulls me by the hand out of the twisty places my mind goes when I'm discouraged. My children—Cassie, Hallie, and Joel—selflessly encourage me to work with schools even when it means I have to leave them, because they know other kids will benefit. My parents, Jeff and Jacki, valued education as I grew up and have supported me unconditionally as an adult. (Even when I wanted to leave a solid journalism job to become a teacher—and when I wanted to leave a solid teaching job to equip and empower teachers.) My deepest thanks to all of you.

ABOUT THE AUTHOR

Matt Miller taught in public schools for more than ten years, teaching all levels of high school Spanish. Over his career, he planned nearly twelve thousand lessons. He taught more than half a million instructional minutes. And he graded work for nearly two thousand days of class.

He is the author of four books, a podcast host, a YouTuber (of sorts), and a relentless sharer on social media. His *Ditch That Textbook* book and blog have equipped and inspired tens of thousands of educators in more than one hundred countries. He holds a master of education from Indiana State University. He's a Google Certified Innovator, a Skype Master Teacher, and the winner of the WTHI-TV Golden Apple award.

At his home in west-central Indiana, he is living the dream: happily married with three kids, two dogs, and a mortgage.

BRING MATT TO YOUR SCHOOL OR EVENT

When you invite Matt to present at your school, district, or event, you'll see results. Teachers use his practical ideas in the classroom the next day. His workshops and conference breakout sessions are hands-on. Teachers learn new ideas for the classroom and practice them firsthand so they're ready to implement. They come away infused with pedagogy, brain science, and inspiration, going far beyond the passive, check-out-this-cool-website–style of professional development.

> "You know it's good stuff when you aren't excited to take a break from learning to eat lunch." —Workshop participant via Twitter

> "This was a day you walk away excited and trying to figure out what you're going to try first!" —Workshop participant via Twitter

After Matt's keynote speeches, educators see their mission in education differently and are ready to claim it. He tells his own story

of ditching his textbooks—including the struggles and doubt. He uses the whole stage, performing his speech with props, costume, and acting techniques. He encourages teachers to take risks, grow through their experiences, and create the classroom of their dreams. Just as important, he helps teachers see how vital they are and how much the world depends on them.

> "Listening to Matt this morning was music to my ears!!! Thank you for the inspiring talk!!!" —Keynote attendee via Twitter

> "Thank you @jmattmiller for the inspiration to be a maverick teacher!" —Keynote attendee via Twitter

FOR MORE INFORMATION ABOUT MATT'S PRESENTATIONS AND SPEECHES, SEND AN E-MAIL TO HELLO@DITCHTHATTEXTBOOK.COM.

MORE FROM

Since 2012, DBCI has published books that inspire and equip educators to be their best. For more information on our titles or to purchase bulk orders for your school, district, or book study, visit **DaveBurgessConsulting.com/DBCIbooks**.

More from *the Like a PIRATE*™ Series

Teach Like a PIRATE by Dave Burgess
eXPlore Like a Pirate by Michael Matera
Learn Like a Pirate by Paul Solarz
Play Like a Pirate by Quinn Rollins
Run Like a Pirate by Adam Welcome

Lead Like a PIRATE™ Series

Lead Like a PIRATE by Shelley Burgess and Beth Houf
Balance Like a Pirate by Jessica Cabeen, Jessica Johnson, and
    Sarah Johnson
Lead beyond Your Title by Nili Bartley
Lead with Appreciation by Amber Teamann and Melinda Miller
Lead with Culture by Jay Billy
Lead with Instructional Rounds by Vicki Wilson
Lead with Literacy by Mandy Ellis

Leadership & School Culture

Culturize by Jimmy Casas
Escaping the School Leader's Dunk Tank by Rebecca Coda and
    Rick Jetter
From Teacher to Leader by Starr Sackstein
The Innovator's Mindset by George Couros
It's OK to Say "They" by Christy Whittlesey

Kids Deserve It! by Todd Nesloney and Adam Welcome

Live Your Excellence by Jimmy Casas

Let Them Speak by Rebecca Coda and Rick Jetter

The Limitless School by Abe Hege and Adam Dovico

Next-Level Teaching by Jonathan Alsheimer

The Pepper Effect by Sean Gaillard

The Principled Principal by Jeffrey Zoul and Anthony McConnell

Relentless by Hamish Brewer

The Secret Solution by Todd Whitaker, Sam Miller, and Ryan Donlan

Start. Right. Now. by Todd Whitaker, Jeffrey Zoul, and Jimmy Casas

Stop. Right. Now. by Jimmy Casas and Jeffrey Zoul

Teach Your Class Off by CJ Reynolds

They Call Me "Mr. De" by Frank DeAngelis

Unmapped Potential by Julie Hasson and Missy Lennard

Word Shift by Joy Kirr

Your School Rocks by Ryan McLane and Eric Lowe

Technology & Tools

50 Things You Can Do with Google Classroom by Alice Keeler and Libbi Miller

50 Things to Go Further with Google Classroom by Alice Keeler and Libbi Miller

140 Twitter Tips for Educators by Brad Currie, Billy Krakower, and Scott Rocco

Block Breaker by Brian Aspinall

Code Breaker by Brian Aspinall

Google Apps for Littles by Christine Pinto and Alice Keeler

Master the Media by Julie Smith

Reality Bytes by Christine Lion-Bailey, Jesse Lubinsky, and Micah Shippee, PhD

Shake Up Learning by Kasey Bell

Social LEADia by Jennifer Casa-Todd

Stepping up to Google Classroom by Alice Keeler and Kimberly Mattina

Teaching Math with Google Apps by Alice Keeler and Diana Herrington

Teachingland by Amanda Fox and Mary Ellen Weeks

Teaching Methods & Materials

All 4s and 5s by Andrew Sharos

Boredom Busters by Katie Powell

The Classroom Chef by John Stevens and Matt Vaudrey

The Collaborative Classroom by Trevor Muir

Copyrighteous by Diana Gill

Ditch That Homework by Matt Miller and Alice Keeler

Ditch That Textbook by Matt Miller

Don't Ditch That Tech by Matt Miller, Nate Ridgway, and Angelia Ridgway

EDrenaline Rush by John Meehan

Educated by Design by Michael Cohen, The Tech Rabbi

The EduProtocol Field Guide by Marlena Hebern and Jon Corippo

The EduProtocol Field Guide: Book 2 by Marlena Hebern and Jon Corippo

Instant Relevance by Denis Sheeran

LAUNCH by John Spencer and A.J. Juliani

Make Learning MAGICAL by Tisha Richmond

Pure Genius by Don Wettrick

The Revolution by Darren Ellwein and Derek McCoy

Shift This! by Joy Kirr

Skyrocket Your Teacher Coaching by Michael Cary Sonbert

Spark Learning by Ramsey Musallam

Sparks in the Dark by Travis Crowder and Todd Nesloney

Table Talk Math by John Stevens

The Wild Card by Hope and Wade King

The Writing on the Classroom Wall by Steve Wyborney

Inspiration, Professional Growth & Personal Development

Be REAL by Tara Martin

Be the One for Kids by Ryan Sheehy

The Coach ADVenture by Amy Illingworth

Creatively Productive by Lisa Johnson

Educational Eye Exam by Alicia Ray

The EduNinja Mindset by Jennifer Burdis

Empower Our Girls by Lynmara Colón and Adam Welcome

Finding Lifelines by Andrew Grieve and Andrew Sharos

The Four O'Clock Faculty by Rich Czyz

How Much Water Do We Have? by Pete and Kris Nunweiler

P Is for Pirate by Dave and Shelley Burgess

A Passion for Kindness by Tamara Letter

The Path to Serendipity by Allyson Apsey

Sanctuaries by Dan Tricarico

The SECRET SAUCE by Rich Czyz

Shattering the Perfect Teacher Myth by Aaron Hogan

Stories from Webb by Todd Nesloney

Talk to Me by Kim Bearden

Teach Better by Chad Ostrowski, Tiffany Ott, Rae Hughart, and Jeff Gargas

Teach Me, Teacher by Jacob Chastain

Teach, Play, Learn! by Adam Peterson

TeamMakers by Laura Robb and Evan Robb

Through the Lens of Serendipity by Allyson Apsey

The Zen Teacher by Dan Tricarico

Children's Books

Beyond Us by Aaron Polansky

Cannonball In by Tara Martin

Dolphins in Trees by Aaron Polansky

I Want to Be a Lot by Ashley Savage

The Princes of Serendip by Allyson Apsey

The Wild Card Kids by Hope and Wade King

Zom-Be a Design Thinker by Amanda Fox

CPSIA information can be obtained
at www.ICGtesting.com
Printed in the USA
BVHW051751250123
657139BV00024B/661